To new beginnings!
Jean Paré

Jean Paré

AN APPETITE
FOR LIFE

**The inspiring story of Canada's most
popular cookbook author**

by Judy Schultz

Company's
Coming

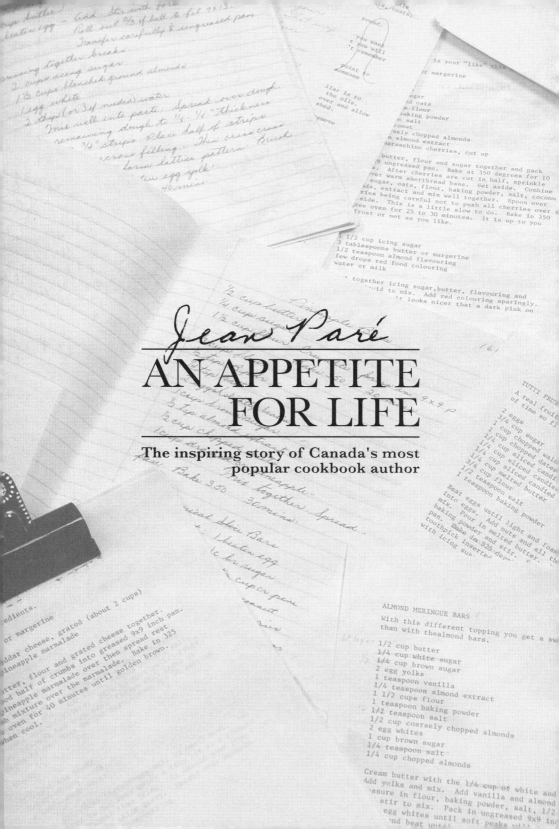

Jean Paré

AN APPETITE FOR LIFE

The inspiring story of Canada's most popular cookbook author

Jean Paré: An Appetite for Life

Copyright © Company's Coming Publishing Limited

All rights reserved worldwide. No part of this book may be reproduced, stored in a retrieval system or transmitted in any form by any means without written permission in advance from the publisher.

In the case of photocopying or other reprographic copying, a license may be purchased from the Canadian Copyright Licensing Agency (Access Copyright). Visit www.accesscopyright.ca or call toll free 1-800-893-5777. In the United States, please contact the Copyright Clearance Centre at www.copyright.com or call 978-646-8600.

Brief portions of this book may be reproduced for review purposes, provided credit is given to the source. Reviewers are invited to contact the publisher for additional information.

Second Printing April 2006

Library and Archives Canada Cataloguing in Publication
Schultz, Judy, date
Jean Paré : an appetite for life : the inspiring story of
Canada's most popular cookbook author / Judy Schultz.
(Original series)
Includes index.
ISBN 1-896891-97-7

1. Paré, Jean, date. 2. Cooks–Canada–Biography.
3. Women authors–Biography. 4. Authors, Canadian–20th
century–Biography. I. Title. II. Series.
TX649.P37S38 2006   641.5'092   C2005-906305-X

Published by
Company's Coming Publishing Limited
2311 – 96 Street
Edmonton, Alberta T6N 1G3 Canada
Tel: 780-450-6223   Fax: 780-450-1857
www.companyscoming.com

Company's Coming is a registered trademark owned by
Company's Coming Publishing Limited

Printed in Canada

Although it was difficult to share my life story, I have done so, hoping it can make a difference. To those who feel like giving up - please don't. You can find help; it's out there. A better life is truly within your reach.

Jean Paré
April 2006

CONTENTS

JUDY SCHULTZ

Researching this book was not my first encounter with Jean Paré.

For a few years, we lived in the same town, and I taught in a school her children attended.

Her catering career was just beginning to take off when I moved away. The next time our paths crossed, she had become a bestselling cookbook author with a hugely successful business built on two things she loved to do — cook, and write about it.

My reaction was probably typical: Why didn't I think of that?

In researching her biography, I came to know the woman behind the large glasses, smiling shyly from the back of a bestselling cookbook. And she was different, more than I expected.

As her story unfolded over many cups of coffee and the ever-present bowl of Bridge Mix, I came to know a survivor.

Here was a woman who had watched as the man she loved turned into an abusive alcoholic. A woman who kept her family together as her marriage and her life crumbled around her.

Today, Jean is an example for other women whose dreams and aspirations are challenged by adversity, no matter what it may be.

This is a story of one woman's determination to create her own dreams, and follow them.

What happened to Jean, and how she not only survived it but became a personal and professional success, is a story of courage, compassion, hope and the power of the human spirit to come back from the brink.

Judy Schultz
April 2006

ONE

STARTERS
A life beginning

On a September morning, eight women make their way down a short, steep street in Vermilion, Alberta.

The street is called Paré Drive, after the town's favourite daughter, Jean Paré, a woman whose series of bestselling cookbooks has brought a touch of fame to the town.

Jean's kitchen table was made for a crowd. The women gathering around it are part of the weekly coffee group, and they get together today as they've done almost every week for 35 years, for coffee, conversation and a little snack.

For her friends, nothing but the best. Jean breaks out the good china and gets ready to serve hot mushroom turnovers as conversation flows around the table, ranging from the times Margaret Snelgrove helped Jean cater some wild and woolly parties, to the recent big event known as the Vermilion Agricultural Fair.

Folks who live in Vermilion just call it The Fair, and they wouldn't miss it, not for anything. People who lived here as children show up from other towns, other provinces, even other countries, often with their own children in tow. It's like a three-day, multi-generation reunion. Everybody comes to The Fair.

One of the women points out that it's the best parade she sees, all summer long; that this year, it was bigger than Lloydminster's. Had more floats, she says, and the horse show was better than ever.

For many years, Jean and her husband, Larry Paré, had a favourite parade-watching spot on Railway Avenue. They'd go an hour early to get a parking space, and Jean would always bring a basket of sandwiches and squares, something to tide them over while they waited for the parade.

For her, there's always a bit of déjà vu in the measured passage of floats and farm machinery, memories of another time, when her name was Jean Lovig, and her four children were on a float advertising their family auction business. Her small daughter, Gail, so cute in a cowgirl costume with a tiny whip; baby pigs squealing in a miniature pen; Grant and Lyall with a few friends in kid-sized bleachers, and Brian playing the auctioneer. Just like his dad.

Then there were the years when she ran her own concession, with people lined up for slow-roasted beef-on-a-bun and homemade pie. In some ways, those had been good times, and the fair was part of it.

"Even now, much of it is volunteer labour," she says thoughtfully. "Everybody pays admission, even the mayor."

A big feature of the fair has always been the cooking, canning and baking show, and there's a raft of entries by local good cooks, but the powers that be have long ago given up asking the most famous cook in town to help judge.

Jean knows better. A lot of her friends have entered the show from time to time, pitting their particular culinary skills against all comers. Yeast breads, buns, cakes (chocolate, carrot, spice, marble), pies (pumpkin, apple, you name it), pickles (sweet, dill, mixed), fruit preserves, jams, jellies in tiny perfect jars, winking in the light, carefully wiped of any errant spill or fingermark.

Some of these women still enter their best culinary efforts in the show, proudly totting up their prize ribbons when they win, feeling slightly cranky when they don't.

Wisely, Jean has always declined the judging honour. Her excuse is chocolate.

"If it was chocolate, it would automatically win," she says.

About 175 kilometres southeast of Edmonton, at the point where Highway 14 passes through the village of Irma, a big white sign shaped like a two-storey cottage declares this to be the birthplace of Jean Paré, author of Company's Coming cookbooks.

Today, Irma is home to 440 citizens, give or take a few. It's a place where some of the family names go back four generations, and strangers in town are quickly noticed. But like many small prairie towns, the once-bustling Main Street has begun to lose its lustre as young people move away and business after business closes its doors for the final time.

It was not always like this. Driving north along Main Street, Jean remembers Irma from a different time, when both blocks bustled with commerce. It was also a town that liked to eat well, where harvest suppers, church teas and bake sales brought out its sociability and its appetite.

Once there'd been a bakery and a coffee shop or two in the small town, and long before her time, the Irma Ice Cream Parlor advertised in the *Irma Times*: "Lunches at all hours, fruit in season, special attention to auto parties."

Keefer's Hall showed a movie every Friday night, and Saturday night there was often a dance, with a live band, music pouring out the door, couples coming and going. Anybody not at the dance would be in Jimmy Pond's cafe, run by the two Jimmies, a father-and-son team who had emigrated from China.

At that time, there were three grocery and dry goods stores supplying the growing wants and needs of the surrounding community.

Neither Foxwell's General Store nor J. C. McFarland General Merchandise did their own butchering and meat cutting, but Ed Elford did, in the Irma Trading Company, the store owned by Jean's parents, Ed and Ruby Elford.

It was a big store on the east side of Main, and the sign above the door, "Buy It At Elford's," was Ed's sincere invitation to shoppers.

He was a consummate merchant. Although he'd had other business ventures before he became a grocer, and would have still others after this one, Ed had no problem figuring out what people with their own gardens and often their own cows and chickens might still want to buy at a grocery store. He had the big wheel of Cheddar cheese, but he also carried the long yellow boxes of Velveeta, and he didn't judge, either way.

Elford's was the first store in town to stock instant coffee. During wartime rations, Ed managed to get his hands on hard-to-find luxuries like canned pineapple jam and fruitcake for his customers. He became a butcher and a meat cutter, and built a smokehouse to process his own bacon and hams. When lard was rationed, he rendered pork fat by melting it down over a slow fire, yielding a fine, snow-white leaf lard that local women considered essential for flaky pie crusts.

During the Second World War, when many families had sons on active service in England or France or God-only-knew-where-else, he developed another specialty, packing food parcels for shipment overseas. He even installed a butter-canning machine, so anxious families could include real butter along with the instant coffee in their packages.

Today, there's a different sign over the door of the former Irma Trading Company. New Horizons, it says. It's a social centre for a busy bunch of local seniors, a comfortable place for cutthroat card games and 80th birthday parties, so it fulfils a useful purpose. But Jean remembers it best when it had a different purpose, and a different name.

"Our house," she says, looking critically at a neat brick veranda and a rolling lawn. "It's smaller than I remember. Or maybe it just seems smaller."

Today the house still stands at the north end of Irma's two-block Main Street, as it has since 1928. Tall spruce trees sway in the yard, and a brass plate on the front lawn announces that this was once the home of Jean Paré. The house is now an office, but it's been left open, even though it's Sunday, so she can walk through her childhood home. Remembering out loud, she pats the fireplace with its original oak mantel, and points to the French doors leading to the dining room.

"Every meal except breakfast was in here."

In the backyard, clearly visible from the kitchen window, is her old playhouse, the one Ed built for his daughter, Jean. Evelyn, his other daughter, was four years older, and apparently laid no claim to the playhouse, so it became Jean's own special domain. It was furnished with a miniature stove, a table, apple-box cupboards and bunk beds, and she remembers one magic summer when her best friend Marjorie Webber came and stayed for three whole days and two nights.

"It was important to me that we stayed there, and didn't set foot in the house," she recalls. "Mom would come out and check on us, but we didn't go in. It made it seem like we were away, on a real holiday."

The little girls cooked their own meals, picking whatever they wanted from the garden. Even then, Jean was enchanted with the domestic arts: gardening, cooking, baking. Some people called it work, but for her, it was part art, part science, and she loved it.

Jean was already showing another side of her character, by becoming the town's youngest entrepreneur. On a spring day when she'd picked a pailful of crocuses, she decided to go into business, and went door to door, peddling her small bouquets for whatever the market would bear.

"I didn't have a set price. One woman paid me 10 cents, and at the time, that was a lot of money. With a dime I could buy two chocolate bars, or a movie ticket. I felt like I was rich."

On a sunny afternoon in 1934, seven-year-old Jean and her friend Marjorie are sitting in Ed's car, letting maplebuds melt on their hands.

"If you hold your hand right there, where the sun comes through the window, they'll melt faster," Jean tells her friend. "Then you can lick them off." It's the beginning of a lifelong obsession with chocolate.

The Trading Company is a mother lode of candy, peppermints, gum drops, English toffees and maplebuds, but that doesn't mean that Jean and her three siblings have carte blanche to just waltz in and gobble down the chocolate.

Ruby Elford is strict about such things. On a winter day, she walks the two blocks home from work with one Caramilk bar tucked in the pocket of her sealskin coat. It's minus 30, and by the time she opens the kitchen door, the bar is frozen solid. She watches as her four children break the icy chocolate bar into squares and share it, cherishing every atom of cold-thickened caramel and milk chocolate as it melts in their mouths.

But her discipline didn't stop her youngest daughter from developing a monumental sweet tooth. At Halloween, racing around the town with her treat bag getting fuller by the minute, Jean considered apples to be a poor substitute for candy, especially as she had fruit every day, thanks to her father's grocery business. Like any self-respecting child, she would trade the scorned apples or give them away at the first opportunity. Just bring on the candy, especially if it was chocolate.

From the day she was born, December 7, 1927, Ed Elford doted on his daughter, Jean, as he did on his other daughter, Evelyn, and his sons, Havie and eventually Ted, who was eight years younger than Jean.

Ed understood children. In a way, he was still a kid at heart. At Easter, he'd get a flock of baby chicks, dyed rainbow colours, and they'd be tumbling around in the front window of his store, green and blue, yellow and purple. Everybody in town came to Elford's to see the chicks, even those who usually shopped at Foxwell's or McFarland's.

At Christmas, Ed would set up an electric train, complete with mountain tunnels and flashing signals. One Christmas, he imported Irma's first and only monkey, a slightly crazy animal that made a lasting impression in a town where the previous most exotic wildlife had been a salamander caught down at the river.

As the Dirty '30s rolled over the prairie, the farming community of Irma began to suffer quietly. Ed Elford was a man who found it impossible to refuse help to a neighbour, and in Irma that included just about everybody. His customers charged their groceries, and he couldn't ask them for money he knew they didn't have, so the bills piled up.

But the wholesalers he dealt with in Edmonton demanded cash, and things got tight at the Irma Trading Company.

The Elford kids, too young to know or care about a Depression that had brought much of the adult world to its financial knees, had been saving for a pony.

"All three of us saved," Jean remembers. "We really wanted that pony, and we had $29. A lot of money, at that time. One day Dad told us he needed to borrow our pony fund. We were out of coal, and he needed cash, so that's where the money went."

The Elford children never got their pony, but neither did they feel deprived. If the '30s were hard days for Ed and Ruby, Jean only realized it in retrospect.

"We still ate well, and we were each allowed one fruit every day, either an orange or an apple. Bananas came home when they were too ripe to sell, and Mom would slice them into a flat dish of Jell-O, so the pieces were spread out and everybody got some fruit. I still enjoy a good jellied salad."

Given the outward prosperity of their store, the Elfords may have looked better off than most folks in their farming community, but there was no money to throw around. Jean remembers getting one new dress a year, no matter how fast she grew.

The dress was for a special occasion, an event that, all across the prairies, had become a combination talent contest and fashion show — the annual school Christmas concert. Night of all nights, it involved the requisite pageant, seasonal musical numbers, recitations, solos, skits, yards and yards of crepe paper costumes and tinsel halos. As the evening wound down, there'd be a visit from a hastily recruited Santa Claus, complete with fluffy cotton whiskers and bags of candy, one for each child.

Every little girl in Irma hoped for a new dress for the big night, and hard times or not, Jean always got one, sewn especially for her.

"We picked out material from the store," she remembers. "Marjorie Webber's mom would sew it for me."

While crops dried out and grasshoppers chewed through what was left, leaving some families all but destitute, the Elfords still had a car, a phone and shiny lino on the floors of their comfortable house. As far as Jean was concerned, life was good, and she was already learning about the pleasures of setting a fine table and cooking delicious things for friends and family.

"We had company almost every Sunday," she recalls. "Sunday School, and then company. Other times we'd be invited out for a meal, because people were careful to reciprocate. It was expected, and having people at your table for a meal was entertainment, long before we had television."

After dinner the men would retire to the living room, where in summer they'd discuss the state of the crops, and in winter, recent government foibles at every level, municipal, provincial and federal.

Meanwhile, the women would clear the table and gather in the kitchen to wash dishes, exchange recipes and discuss local happenings. As far as Jean was concerned, the jokes and gentle gossip in the kitchen were also part of the entertainment, nearly as important as the meal itself. She never had a problem with the none-too-subtle segregation. She knew who was having the most fun.

Jean, at nine or ten, is happily presiding over a tea party by the playhouse. Her blonde hair is windblown, her small face animated. Her younger brother, Ted, and her best friend, Marjorie, wait expectantly for treats.

"Mom was always baking. We had a coal and wood stove, and I knew if I could hold my arm in the oven for a few seconds, it was just right for a cake. If it nearly burned the fuzz off my arm, it was hot enough for a pie. That's how we knew. Early on, Mom made the pastry and I filled the pies."

The usual batch was six pies. It was a time when pies were an essential part of a woman's domestic arts, and her homemaking skills and reputation as a cook were judged on the flakiness of her pastry.

Thanks in part to the excellent leaf lard from Ed's rendering business, Ruby Elford excelled in pie crust, rolling out a batch of never-fail pastry every Saturday, so there'd be pie for the onslaught of Sunday company.

She waited eagerly for rhubarb and saskatoons in June, strawberries in July for her famous double-crust strawberry pie, Okanagan peaches in August, green apples in September. During the Depression, some women filled their pies with sour cream and raisins; with mashed carrots, which tasted just like pumpkin; with mock mincemeat, made with green tomatoes and apples. If wartime shortages or tight budgets left them without fresh lemons, they could make a darn good vinegar pie.

Most of the time in those pre-Saran, pre-refrigerator days, Ruby stuck with double-crust pies, because they were better keepers. Except for a family favourite, sour cream and raisin, she avoided most cream pies, because they spoiled so fast.

Fruit pies were another matter. They were reliable. You could put a double-crust fruit pie in the cool of the north-facing back porch, covered with a dinner plate to ward off any passing flies, and it would keep for three days, maybe four. In winter, the porch became a walk-in freezer, and cookies and cakes would freeze beautifully.

The Elford home and its reliable hospitality became a beacon for the legion of unemployed men riding the rails during the lean years of the '30s. Somehow word got around, and when the train slowed down for Irma, they'd jump off a freight at one end of Main Street and head straight for the Elfords' butter-coloured house at the other end.

"I guess we called them hobos, but they were just hungry men without jobs. Mom fed them all, and they'd work a little in return, maybe chopping wood, but it was mostly for their own dignity. She never turned anybody away. She never would have."

When Jean flew through the kitchen door after school, she usually had a friend in tow. Their particular target was the cookie jar, for a handful of Ruby's hermits or peanut butter cookies. On baking days, the girls would butter thick slices of fresh bread and dunk them, butter-side down, in the sugar drawer, letting the excess run off the bread and leaving the odd telltale crumb in the sugar.

"Mom bought sugar in 20-pound sacks, and it was stored in that special drawer so it was handy for baking. I was always getting heck for leaving crumbs in the sugar. Havie did the same thing. Not Evelyn though."

Evelyn was older than Jean, and given her years, maybe wiser.

With the warm golden days of midsummer came canning season, when wooden cases of plums and pears with gorgeous, painted labels would be stacked near the counter in Elford's, and the air would smell sweetly of ripening fruit. Jean loved the way the stone fruit was packed, with squares of tissue-thin paper wrapped around each individual peach or apricot and twisted at the top, to close it, as though it was a gift.

The store got so busy that Ruby would take Jean out of school early, so she could help serve customers, and that was nothing but fun. It made her feel grown up and important.

"Every woman in town canned her own fruit, and a lot of them bought it from my dad. All summer long the fruit kept coming. Cherries were first, in late June, and after that he'd buy raspberries, strawberries and loganberries from B.C., but blueberries were wild. They came from some pickers near Bonnyville."

Then the fruit trucks would come rumbling in from the Okanagan with the last of the stone fruit, the green pie apples and the first of the new Macs, the shiny red apples that had such a wonderful perfume. Even to a child who prefers chocolate to fruit, nothing smells quite so good as a new-crop Mac.

At the time, Ruby was working long hours in the store as well as running her household, raising her three children (later to be four) and caring for two of her husband's aged relatives, Great Aunt Alice Weir, and Alice's sister, Grandmother Lindsay.

The two old ladies lived upstairs, ruling the second floor with their presence, blissfully unaware that they made so much extra work for Ruby. Extra laundry, extra cleaning, extra attention in so many ways. Then there were all the tray meals to be carried up to Grandma Lindsay, who seldom came downstairs, but spent much of her time in nightgown and nightcap, peering out the upstairs bedroom window at the woodpile where, she was certain, there were evil intruders waiting to pounce.

On the prairies, there were very few of what more affluent parts of the country called domestic servants, but in small towns there was often one person in a household known only, and always, as the hired girl. Part cook, part housemaid, part laundress and if need be, babysitter, the hired girl was usually young, with few dreams beyond the possibility of a lucky marriage to one of the local boys.

In the Elford house, it was the hired girl's job to take the extra work off Ruby's shoulders, helping care for the elderly women upstairs and doing a few other household duties. Ruby could then find those hours she needed to play piano for the Sunday School and lead a United Church girls' youth group.

But neither Jean nor her older sister, Evelyn, was fond of the arrangement.

"I always resented the hired girls," Jean says. "I don't really know why, except maybe they were a bit bossy and I was pretty independent. I didn't need some strange girl moving in and taking over. Maybe I was just an ornery kid.

"Finally my sister and I told Mom we were old enough to manage the household ourselves, so Mom said we'd have to divide the work, and I chose cooking. At twelve, I could make a pretty good chocolate cake with date filling, and I made it often. It was Dad's favourite cake, and if he or anybody else got tired of my cooking, they never said so."

Jean was a natural cook. There was an instinct. Given a choice between cooking and playing with other kids, she'd likely choose cooking. After school she and Evelyn would often whip up a batch of fudge, and Havie liked to get involved. On Saturday, there were always those six pies to be made for Sunday, because there'd be company coming.

The Sunday company was never in doubt and, at that time in history, the parties were always dry.

Prohibition had kept Alberta pure as the driven snow from 1918 to 1926, and the United Church, a combination of Methodist and Presbyterian from Central and Eastern Canada, maintained their own brand of prohibition after that. Jean's family were church-going teetotallers.

"We didn't start a meal with appetizers. We were in a small town, where things like appetizers and pre-dinner cocktails were not yet the thing to do." The Canadian wine industry was still in the sweet sherry stage, and even if they'd wanted a bottle of wine with their meal, they'd have had very slim pickings.

Still, the Elfords maintained a certain style, and Jean remembers that on special occasions, they had grape juice or tomato juice served in stemmed crystal glasses before the main course.

"The fancy glasses made it special."

The Elford family year was marked by certain celebrations: Easter, Thanksgiving, Christmas. Each one brought with it certain rituals involving food.

At Christmas, everyone would be at the Elford's for a huge turkey-smelling noon dinner, with a giant bird roasted to a deep mahogany brown, a rich gravy, a bread stuffing, two vegetables, jellied salads, cranberries and all the other trimmings. A second hot meal was served for supper, when they warmed up the turkey, the stuffing and all the vegetables.

"Neither meal was small, and there was a proper steamed pudding for dessert after dinner, with brown sugar sauce," says Jean. "The mince pies came after supper."

At New Year's, however, the whole family went to the Locke's for a meal that was a touch more formal.

Jean's grandparents, Arthur and Amy Locke, lived in a large, imposing house one street away. Having come from Prince Edward Island, where so many fortunes were made in fox ranching, Arthur still kept a few foxes, and Jean remembers their cages behind the garden.

The Lockes also had the luxury of a refrigerator, and she loved to spread cold butter on thick slices of homemade bread, and dunk it in cold molasses.

"We always had New Year's dinner at Grandma Locke's, and it was served in the evening. Grandad sat at the head of the table, and he would carve the turkey, asking each of us what we wanted. Of course everybody wanted the wishbone."

Even though it was the middle of winter, Grandad Locke always made his special out-of-season ice cream for dessert, packing the wooden freezer with ice and salt, and turning the crank until it was so stiff it wouldn't go another round, which meant the ice cream was ready.

"It was vanilla, made with a cooked custard base, and it was delicious. There were no limits that night — we were allowed to have all the ice cream we wanted."

Jean's mother had exquisite china and silver, inherited from the Elford side, but her grandmother Locke's tables were also works of domestic art.

"Grandma loved setting a pretty table. She also had beautiful china and silver, and I remember all the salad forks, the tiny coffee spoons, the gravy ladles. There were very small containers of nuts and mints by each plate on those occasions. I thought it was extremely elegant, and very special."

TWO

SALAD DAYS
On being young and green

Jean was only twelve when a crazy little man named Adolph Hitler plunged the world into a second great war with Germany.

Europe and Britain went on food rations immediately, and Ottawa soon printed ration books for Canadians, restricting meats, fats, sugar and other luxury goods, but in Irma, Alberta, nobody was losing sleep over food rationing.

"We stopped taking sugar on cereal and in tea, but it was mostly a gesture of loyalty. There were no real shortages," Jean recalls. "Mom still baked every week. Local farm women would try to trade eggs and butter for groceries, but we made our own butter. We had a cow and two gardens, and I used to feed the cow beets, just because she liked them."

When Jean started working in the Trading Company every day after school, she was stimulated by all the comings and goings, the constant chatter, the polite visiting, the discussion around the news of the day and the odd snippet of juicy gossip that went on across the counter. It was a sociable job, and a shy child could feel included.

Jean's help in the store was valued, especially by her mother, Ruby, because there were days when Ruby had other fish to fry. She had an unusual skill for a woman at that time: she knew how to drive a car, and was good at it. She loved taking to the road.

Ruby was the first woman in the Irma district to have a driver's licence, and when the RCMP came to town to look for illegal stills tucked away in the surrounding hills, it was often Ruby who acted as their chauffeur.

Maybe it was the possibility of something extra in an ordinary life, but she seized every opportunity to drive.

She also enjoyed alfresco meals. On hot summer Sundays in July and August, Ruby would pack up a lunch and she and Ed would drive the kids 10 miles to the banks of the Battle River, near the village of Fabyan.

Today the Battle is a slow, shallow waterway, hardly more than a creek in some places, cutting a mud-brown swath through the midsummer green of the valley, but in years of heavy snow and ample rain it gets broader and deeper, becoming once more the swimmable stream of Ruby's time.

At a spot not far out of the village, her children had a favourite swimming hole with a sandy beach on the other side. Not exactly a babbling brook, but it was cool and wet. Jean was allowed to take a friend, and after the swim there'd be a picnic.

"Mom always made potato salad, and we'd eat it with pork and beans and canned Vienna sausage or a can of Prem, a popular brand of spiced pork that we heated on a gas camp stove. You needed a tin key to open the can, and it was supposed to be stuck on the lid. Sometimes the key would have gone missing, and then you had an awful time getting the can opened.

"When the war came and the soldiers started using the swimming hole to go skinny-dipping, we stopped going. They only got two showers a week, so we figured they needed the swim more than we did! Not that we had a choice, because they weren't about to leave."

So far, the war hadn't meant a lot to Jean and her friends, one way or the other, but gradually, even in Irma, there were signs that their world was changing, and might never be quite the same again.

"The men would come into Irma from Camp Wainwright, and they'd travel in a convoy of trucks and jeeps and park all along the road. It was exciting, somehow, just seeing them there. I remember one guy on a motorbike. He was a military policeman, and that impressed me.

"On Saturday nights they'd come to town for the dance, and often they'd ask if they could park their jeeps behind the trees in our yard. They were always very polite — they'd just knock on the door and ask. We never locked our doors, and in those days we never worried about strangers who came knocking."

The war dragged on, and one day in December 1941, Jean came bounding down the stairs, expecting some degree of hoopla. After all, it was December 7, her birthday, and normally that was cause for celebration.

But the day Jean turned fourteen, the Japanese bombed Pearl Harbour, and Ruby and Ed were so engrossed with what they were hearing that they kept the radio turned up all day.

"They had their ears so glued to that radio, they almost forgot it was my birthday," she says, sounding a touch miffed even now.

Maybe it was her contact with adults through the store that did it, but Jean was already developing a feisty streak. She's never forgotten a certain farmer coming into the store with his cream cheque, or how she instinctively disliked his attitude toward his wife and family.

"Dad would cash his cheque for him, and this guy would always buy tobacco, for his roll-your-owns. If there was money left over after that, he'd hem and haw and finally say, 'I guess I'll get some flour for the wife,'" she recalls, still bristling.

"Flour, for the wife. After all the cooking and baking she had to do for him and his brood of kids, he acted like a bag of flour was some kind of special gift, and she should be grateful. I'd have fed that man sawdust!"

Nobody, least of all Jean, could have known how important that feisty, independent spirit was to become in her own survival.

Two guys and two girls are standing on a stage with musical instruments: piano, drums, clarinet … Jean, her hair now curly, is holding her newly acquired treasure, a C-melody saxophone.

"I was sixteen, and I loved music, so my folks bought me a C-melody saxophone, one my uncle had. I figured I could teach myself to play, and I just got busy and did it."

It took Jean a month to play well enough to form a band, the Ink Spots, with friends Shirley Thomson on piano, Carl Soneff on clarinet and Jack Fletcher on drums.

Later, the band became The Five Flats, with Evelyn on piano, her brother-in-law Charlie on drums, Jean and Havie on sax, and Carl still on clarinet. The Five Flats became a big hit on the weekend dance circuit, playing in country schools all around Irma, Hardisty and Wainwright.

In the Mood; Ma! I Miss Your Apple Pie; The Beer Barrel Polka; and their all-time biggest hit, *Tiger Rag.*

"The first time we played *Tiger Rag*, nobody danced. We got worried, but when we were finished, everybody applauded! We did all the war songs. We followed the hit parade, we'd take requests, and we all sang."

Although food rationing barely caused a ripple, the war had brought other changes to the sleepy farming towns of central Alberta. Farmers and townsfolk watched their young men go off to fight in Europe, and suddenly men in uniform became a common sight on the main streets of modest burgs like Irma, and bigger ones like Vermilion. They all came from the military base at Camp Wainwright, lonely farm boys away from home for the first time, but there's something about a uniform that gives a man a certain sophistication, no matter where he's from, or how shy and lonely he may be.

"Camp Wainwright really smartened those Irma boys up," Jean recalls. "When I wasn't playing my saxophone, I danced, and I'd book my dances ahead, but never more than three."

Jean danced with a lot of soldiers, and listened to a lot of lines about how cute she was, what a good dancer she was, and how much they liked being with her. Some of the boys brought her gifts, and she accumulated quite a collection of silk scarves.

"They'd say, 'I'm being shipped overseas. Will you write to me?' They were just homesick, and maybe scared, and of course I'd say yes. I'd write for awhile, but there was never anything in my letters he couldn't show his mother," she says primly.

The soldiers she danced with in Keefer's Hall or the country schools where The Five Flats played were never more than a temporary fling. Sometimes, too temporary.

"There were some who didn't come back. For awhile, Canadian paratroopers over France or Belgium were being shot out of the sky like geese. I never heard from some of them again, and I assumed they'd been killed, or taken prisoner. It happened too often.

"There was one who wrote until he got to Belgium, but then the letters stopped. I thought … well, I never expected he'd be coming home."

But he did, and years later, when he was safely back in Canada with a Belgian war bride, their paths crossed again.

"Somebody told me he was living in Blue Ridge, Alberta, so I sent him a Christmas card and just signed it 'Clarence and Jean Lovig,' because I was married by that time."

The next Christmas, he sent her a card, with a note: "Who ARE you?"

She kept him on her Christmas list, and signed the next card "Clarence and Jean (Elford) Lovig."

The following summer, a stranger pulled up in a gasoline truck and introduced himself to Jean.

"Remember me?"

"I didn't recognize him at all," she says. "In his work clothes, he looked nothing like the soldier I knew."

It was an experience shared by a lot of women who had met men in smart military uniforms, and were surprised to see how very ordinary those same men looked once the uniform had been hung away in the closet.

Then there was Jimmy Sharky, a local boy who'd sent word home to Irma that on a certain day he'd be going through town on a troop train.

"They were special trains full of soldiers heading all the way to Halifax, and their schedules were supposed to be top secret. The troop trains didn't stop, didn't even slow down, but the word seemed to get around when one would be coming through. This time we all went down to watch, to see if Jimmy would be looking out a window, and we could all wave."

Jimmy did better than that. Not content with a wave, he was standing on the rear platform of the last car, and when the train thundered past, he raised his pitching arm like any baseball-playing prairie boy would do, and threw a half-eaten apple into the crowd.

Tied to it was a note for his dad.

"Jimmy made it home too," she says. "But a lot of them didn't. Or, they came home in awful shape, even if you couldn't see what was wrong. Those were the ones that still had their arms and legs, but they were terribly affected in other ways. We called it shell shock then. Now, I think it's post-traumatic stress."

On a warm May morning in the spring of 1945, the most exciting news began spreading through the town of Irma: Germany had surrendered. Hitler was finished.

They'd waited six long years for this. The war in Europe was over, VE Day had arrived, and it was time to celebrate.

The Five Flats were booked to play for a dance in Keefer's Hall that night, and the whole town turned out for the party.

"Play *In the Mood*. Play *Happy Days Are Here Again!*"

On VE Day, the streets of Paris and London were filled with jubilant crowds, singing, laughing, kissing anybody and everybody.

In Halifax and Dartmouth, several thousand sailors and civilians got roaring drunk and a mob surged through the streets, smashing windows and destroying property. Their party went down in history as the infamous VE Day riots.

In Irma, they just kept on dancing.

"Everybody was so happy it was finally over. The boys were coming home. Most of them, anyway.

"Someone passed a hat and asked us to keep playing. So we played, and they danced, until the sun came up."

Oddly enough, considering her active social life, the man in Jean's immediate future wasn't a soldier.

He was a local boy who'd been discharged from the army because of a perforated eardrum, and he'd been right there on Main Street, all the time.

Clarence Lovig was one of fourteen children born to Olaf and Sanna Lovig, a Norwegian couple who lived on a farm not far out of town.

They were hard-living people with few resources, and there was not much doubt that Sanna Lovig had her hands full with such a big family. But when company came to the Lovig farm, they'd kill a couple of chickens for supper, dig a couple of hills of potatoes, and make everyone welcome around the table.

Clarence worked as a gas jockey and part-time mechanic at Ostad's, the garage on the corner owned by his brother-in-law.

Clarence was one of those lean, bad-boy types that just naturally make female hearts beat faster. He was handsome, cocky, a snappy dresser — white shirt and tie, and a rakish tilt to a snap-brimmed felt hat, later to be exchanged for his trademark Stetson. He loved to laugh, to have a sociable drink, to be the life of the party. He was also, in Jean's words, the best dancer in the world, and her own love of music and dancing wasn't lost on him. Here was a girl who could be a lot of fun.

When she walked by the garage on her way to the store, he talked to her, teased her, flirted with her. Jean was a cute kid, and although she was eight years younger than Clarence and a bit on the shy side, that, too, appealed to him.

It was only natural that she would enjoy the attentions of a handsome, charismatic older man like Clarence. By the time she was sixteen she had blossomed into a pretty young woman, and the flirting got serious. Jean was falling in love, and there wasn't a thing she or anybody else could do to stop it. She fell hard, hopelessly and completely.

Some girls might have started a hope chest, or spent hours composing lyrical prose in a five-year diary.

Jean took a more practical view. She wrote her first cookbook: sat down and copied all of Ruby's best recipes into a scribbler. Fried chicken, hamburgers in milk gravy, Swiss steak, all the good rib-sticking dishes a man would want to come home to after a hard day.

It was a time and place when lunch was something you took to school in a honey pail if you lived on a farm. Otherwise, at home, dinner was a hot meal, cooked and served at noon, and the leftovers were heated up for supper at six o'clock, or whenever the resident breadwinner strode through the door.

Neither the noon dinner nor evening supper could end properly without dessert, so she copied those too: brown Betty, made with apples; the sweet-and-spicy tomato soup cake; matrimonial cake with a buttery oatmeal crust; light-as-feathers angel cake for days when there were extra eggs. A pan of smog bars would always be good to have with coffee, and when they had company coming, there'd be deep apple pie.

She wrote them all down.

"I intended to marry him," she says. "I needed my recipes."

THREE

IN THE SOUP
I'm swimming as fast as I can

Ed and Ruby Elford weren't exactly overjoyed with their youngest daughter's plans to marry the local ladies' man, but they were too smart to dismiss her intentions, or to lay down any stern parental law and forbid her to see him. Instead, they managed to talk the strong-willed teenager into finishing school before launching herself into eternal wedded bliss.

"Clarence came to work for Dad. He learned to butcher meat and cut it up properly, and he was really very good in the store," she recalls, and then adds thoughtfully, "He was always good with people."

The truth was that Clarence had many good points, and to his credit, he tried hard to improve himself, even asking Jean to correct his grammar whenever he made a mistake.

Still, her parents held out, and although she graduated from high school at seventeen, Jean had to wait until December, and her eighteenth birthday, before they'd agree to their daughter making wedding plans.

Then one day, very soon after her birthday, it was official.

"Clarence sold his car. That's how serious he was! We bought an engagement ring and wedding rings, and I caught a ride to Edmonton with a traveller, to buy my wedding clothes."

Jean's mother had given her $25 to buy her wedding dress, a practical pale blue crepe two-piece, and a smart navy blue suit for travelling.

Late on a February afternoon in 1946, the United Church minister, the Reverend H. W. Inglis, arrived at the Elford home to perform a quiet wedding ceremony.

"We didn't have a big wedding. It was just the times. The war was recently over. My folks didn't have much money. Neither did Clarence and I."

Jean's memories of her wedding to Clarence are oddly fuzzy, and considering how important weddings and wedding parties would later become to her professional life, she kept things simple.

"There weren't many people there, just family," she recalls. "My family, and some of Clarence's people, probably no more than two dozen altogether. We must have had a supper afterward, like a very small reception, though I can't remember what we ate."

Jean was also too excited to notice the wedding cake, but it was almost certainly a dark fruitcake, the traditional western Canadian wedding cake of the day. Such cakes were always rich and heavy, often laced with rum, and full of raisins, glacé fruit, walnuts and almonds. They were baked in tiers, with the top tier well wrapped and saved for the christening party after the birth of a first child. The other layers were for cutting, and legend promised that unmarried girls who slept with a piece of wedding cake tucked under their pillows would dream of their future husbands.

For whatever reason, neither Ruby, nor the about-to-be-married Jean, nor her older sister Evelyn took a stab at baking the wedding cake, so Ed picked one up in Edmonton and brought it home just before the event.

"After the supper party, my sister Evelyn and her husband drove us to Wainwright to catch the Midnight Flyer for Saskatoon. We couldn't afford a berth, so we sat up all night on the train, and then changed trains for Regina."

The wedding breakfast would have been simple.

"You could get coffee and sandwiches on the train in those days."

They visited some of Clarence's relations near Regina, but a few days later the honeymoon was over and they were back in Irma, moving into a two-room house rented from Jean's grandfather.

Clarence, standing tall, scoops a young Jean into his arms. She smiles, but her posture is uncomfortable, as though she's afraid he might drop her.

Their first son, Lyall, arrived in August of 1947. Jean was able to see a doctor only twice before he was born.

"We had to borrow Dad's car in order to get there, and the doctor was 22 miles away."

Lyall, who slept in a wicker clothes basket until Jean's parents presented him with a crib, was a happy, healthy baby and Jean loved being a mother.

Baby Lyall, dressed in his birthday finery, is speeding on hands and knees toward his birthday cake. It's a chiffon cake, the one that will always be associated with family celebrations.

That same year, her parents sold the Irma Trading Company and bought the Rock Oil Company warehouse in Edmonton. Their entire close-knit family moved to the city in order to invest in the new business venture. Ed and Ruby bought a house in the Highlands district with a small suite upstairs for Jean and Clarence.

"We had plumbing and natural gas," Jean recalls, pleased even now with such amazing luck.

It was a good time, even though there were shortages. Edmonton was enjoying a rush of post-war prosperity, and the baby boom had started. But the population of young families outstripped the available goods and services, so there were long waiting lists for the simple convenience of a telephone, although pregnant women could have one installed, at least temporarily, before the birth of the baby. Household appliances like washing machines and refrigerators were also hard to come by.

"I'd go for groceries, and the lineups would be so long that by the time I got through the checkout, my ice cream would be dripping."

After the baby was born, Jean decided to start drinking skim milk. In a true sign of the times, the milkman explained that she'd have to get a doctor's prescription before he could sell it to her. Everybody else had to drink whole milk, as part of post-war support for the dairy industry.

About that time Jean had a bit of luck. She'd made a rare find — a good, second-hand refrigerator, so she could keep milk and cream. Finally, things were shaping up in her favourite room — her kitchen.

Meanwhile, Clarence was moving up in the world. He'd gone to work as a salesman for Jean's dad at Rock Oil, and bought himself a car. He hit the road, travelling all week, coming home on weekends.

In August of 1950 their second baby, Brian, was born. Borrowing the down payment from Jean's grandfather, they bought their own two-bedroom house in Edmonton's Virginia Park area, a part of town with tree-lined boulevards and, true to its name, a nearby park. It was the kind of neighbourhood that would be good for children.

"There was a zoo in Borden Park in those days, and the children loved going there. They'd take lettuce and feed the deer, and we'd watch the monkeys. There was a swimming pool too, and Brian was crazy about the water. He'd swim three times a day, if I'd let him."

At the time, Jean's domestic wish list was short and simple.

"We had a wringer washer, a fridge, a garden, a car," she says. "I had a coffee table and a chesterfield suite. Grandad built a suite in our basement, and the rent we got from it made our payments every month."

Jean has always loved the Christmas season, not just for the celebrations around the table, but for the music, the decorating, the Christmas tree. She remembers her third Christmas as Clarence's wife, when they could finally afford a string of eight lights for their small tree.

"For our first Christmas, I made crepe paper decorations. The second year, I think we managed to buy a set of glass balls. By our third Christmas we had lights, and I thought they made it a beautiful tree. They were series lights, and if one light bulb burned out, they all quit working."

In retrospect, the series lights might have been a sort of foreshadowing, a metaphor for Jean's life. But for the moment, all was well.

In 1954 Jean had a third baby boy, and they named him Grant. Clarence moved the family to a second house, this one also in Edmonton's well-established Highlands neighbourhood. They rented out the first house, and bought their first television set.

"The good times were so good," she says wistfully. "We didn't have much, but it didn't seem to matter."

They'd catch a movie on Friday night for 25 cents, have friends over for cards, celebrate birthdays with family dinners and chiffon cakes, one of Jean's favourites for special occasions.

"It was a cake that took seven whole eggs, and it was moist, but firm enough that it could be sliced into sixteen wedges."

Those seven-egg chiffon cakes became her signature birthday cake within the family. It was the mid '50s, and major food companies like Pillsbury and Betty Crocker were doing their bit to free women from kitchen chores by inventing the cake mix. Jean recalls that the first ones were just add-water-and-stir.

"They weren't really very good, a bit on the dry side, like they needed something extra."

So she'd add an egg, or some oil.

Ironically, the earliest mixes weren't a commercial success for that very reason. They needed something extra, and Jean recalls discussions among her cake-baking friends about the relative merits of the various cake mixes.

"I think women, in general, wanted to do more than just add water to a mix, and very soon the formulas changed, and directions started calling for eggs and oil. Gradually, they became almost-from-scratch cakes, but they had better texture than the first mixes and were more like what people expected in a homemade cake," she says.

"I've never had anything against a good cake mix, especially when I'm in a hurry.

"Eventually, Betty Crocker brought out a chiffon cake mix, and it was really a very good cake, but it was only available for a few years. They stopped making them, and I still wonder why."

Cake and coffee, Sunday dinners with her parents, birthday parties for the children. The mid '50s were good for Jean and her family, and in the jargon of the day, a kind of domestic bliss settled over the house in the Edmonton Highlands.

She had everything she'd ever dreamed of. A handsome, loving husband. Three little boys to cuddle. Her own home, with a real kitchen, a place to bake her pies and roast her chickens, and a dining table to serve them on. It was almost like playing house; like old times, back in the Irma days.

Life unfolded sweetly before her, and the future was nothing but a rosy glow, as far as she could see.

October 2004. Jean's sunny office, on the second floor of the Company's Coming building on Edmonton's south side, is like a well-appointed living room in a family home. Chintz loveseat, photographs on a sideboard, a couple of art-quality dolls reposing in a chair.

She picks up a pen from the well-polished desk, puts it down, adjusts a blind, brushes some imagined fluff from her skirt.

Some things are almost too painful to talk about, even now, and her tone, when she speaks, is deliberately flat and controlled.

"One day I found that my name had been taken off our joint bank account."

For a woman as independent as Jean, it was like being slapped, but it was a blow she wouldn't take lightly.

"I can't tell you how very degrading it was to me to have to ask for money," she says, reflecting on the old humiliation.

Deeply hurt by the financial incident, Jean was bewildered by her husband's Jekyll-and-Hyde behaviour. She'd noticed things lately, nothing she could put her finger on, but Clarence had been different, somehow. She'd been trying to ignore it, hoping he'd get over whatever it was that was bothering him, and they'd be able to go back to their old life. But this was serious. This she could not ignore.

However, Jean didn't waste a lot of time brooding. It wasn't her nature to feel sorry for herself. Within days, she'd found a job and hired a babysitter.

Then Clarence came home, and when he discovered that his wife had suddenly become a career woman, he was anything but happy. He flew into a rage and summarily fired the sitter.

"He told her to go home and stay there," she remembers bitterly.

Jean was devastated, but she had three small children to raise, and she decided not to fight him on this.

Her neighbour offered to drive her to the grocery store, so she swallowed her pride and asked Clarence for food money.

He flatly refused to give her anything. Not a nickel. She couldn't understand why.

"Go ahead and starve," he yelled at her. "I don't care if the kids starve, as long as you starve too."

"I knew he didn't mean it about the kids, not really, but it hurt. The next morning he was gone, but he'd left some money on the kitchen table. I sent Lyall off to school, and then I walked with the two little ones four blocks to the bus, bought as much as I could carry, and took the bus back. That's how we got our groceries."

Jean didn't know the first thing about alcohol. Like the rest of her family, she was a teetotaller.

"I didn't have my first drink until I was thirty-three," she muses. "I still remember. It was a horse's neck, made with scotch. I could taste the liquor, and I didn't like it."

But Clarence liked it. He had always enjoyed a social drink, and for some time she'd suspected that he was drinking too much, too often. All those days and nights on the road were changing him, and he was no longer the charming, happy-go-lucky man she'd married, at least not with her.

Now he was angry, suspicious, deceitful. It terrified Jean, but she felt helpless and somehow shamed, so she kept quiet.

Her silence was a mistake she regrets to this day.

When Clarence decided to buy an auction mart in Clover Bar, on the outskirts of Edmonton, Jean thought it was a hopeful sign. He was a good auctioneer, self-taught, and he had a certain charisma, along with a gift for remembering faces and names. Men respected him, women found him charming and attentive.

"Clarence could sell ice to a polar bear," his friends said. "Clarence could charm the birds out of the trees."

With her grandfather's help, Jean ran the coffee shop at the auction mart, and also managed the office, balancing the sales records after each sale.

Once again, she dared to start hoping. Maybe Clarence would stop drinking and be home at night. Maybe everything would be all right after all.

But within a few months, her life once more began to unravel.

"Clarence was drinking again," she says, sighing.

"Not just a sociable beer after work, either. That wouldn't have worried me. But he was drinking heavily. I guess he'd never stopped."

The marriage was getting rocky.

"He'd go to bed when the kids went," she says. "He'd take the two little ones into our bed, so he wouldn't have to be alone with me. We seldom spent time together as a couple. Less and less, as time passed."

In July of 1957 their fourth child, a daughter, Gail, was born. Once again, Jean became a full-time mother. Clarence was at the auction mart all the time, and as bad as his drinking had been, it was getting worse. When he'd come home, he'd fall into bed, apparently too tired even to talk to her.

The closeness they'd once shared was gone. Most of the time, so was he. He had two faces: one affable, hail-fellow-well-met public face; and one sinister, private face, reserved especially for his wife. When she looked at Clarence, Jean no longer liked what she was seeing.

In spite of the drinking, his business seemed to prosper. He sold the auction mart in Clover Bar, then started the Vermilion Auction Mart and later built a sister operation in Vegreville, about an hour's drive east of Edmonton.

In 1959, he told her they were moving to Vermilion so he could be closer to his work. Reluctantly, Jean agreed, but only if he'd sign over the original house on 74th Street, in the Virginia Park district, and put it in her name. For some reason she's never fully understood, he agreed.

"There wasn't a lot of equity," she says. "But it was a bit of security. Somehow, I knew I needed to hang onto that. We'd borrowed the money from my grandfather to buy it so I needed to control the payments. I rented it out when we moved."

That may have been the first time Jean had realized the critical importance of being financially prudent and looking after her own money. It wouldn't be the last.

October 2004. A decisive woman in a well-cut blue suit, Jean glances out her office window and once again her hands move nervously over the desktop, as though looking for something. Answers, maybe. She sighs, because this still hurts, this memory that bothers her most of all, and when she finally speaks, there's a bitter note in her voice.

"After every sale, he'd get so drunk!"

The Yellowhead Highway runs east from Edmonton, and doglegs around Vegreville before it reaches Vermilion. Here the rolling green prairie is scattered with grazing cattle, black Angus, Simmental, Herefords and, now and then, the big white French cattle called Charolais.

Vermilion, a community of several thousand people on the south bank of the river it's named after, is a pretty town, with a broad main street of solid buildings, many of them brick.

People here have done well for themselves. The brick structures are both a mark of the prosperity this town has enjoyed for the past century, and a reminder of one bad day in 1918, when a disastrous fire wiped out most of its existing main street.

In summer, flower baskets hang from the lampposts on Main Street, perfuming the long July evenings. In the early dark of December, Christmas lights twinkle in the windows of Craig's Department Store and Long's Value Drug Mart. All year through, up and down this street, people stop to pass the time of day when they meet.

There was a time when the auction mart on the west side of town was also a meeting place, especially on sale days.

Auction marts have their own excitement, their own rush. Folks in this part of the country say you can smell three things at a good auction: cattle, coffee and cash. The bleachers around the sales ring are full, and as the animals are herded in, the auctioneer is the star of his own show, his singsong patter crackling through the microphone, entertaining the crowd, so even those who aren't buying are having a good time.

Lot 25 now, ladies and gents. We got some fine little bred heifers here, friends. Who'll start the bidding at one-fifty? Thank you sir, I got one-fifty, now two, now two-fifty ... Who'll give me three? Three hundred dollars? Going once for two-fifty, going twice ... all in, all done, SOLD, for two hundred and fifty dollars to my good friend in the black hat.

Clarence was a showman. If he'd had a motto, it would have been "Always leave them laughing," and he had a million tricks to keep the people entertained.

In September, he'd bring in cases of apples and oranges, and throw the fruit into the bleachers for them to catch. At Thanksgiving, he auctioned fresh turkeys for the appreciative crowd, and gave the odd one away, if he knew a man couldn't afford to buy one of the big birds, and had a family to feed.

Before long, Clarence had his own television show, a weekly livestock report on CKSA Lloydminster. It was a half hour during prime time, complete with a country band and celebrity guests, including visiting rodeo clowns.

On a slow day, Clarence would bring the two younger kids on the show, Grant in a fringed cowboy shirt and Stetson, Gail with a basket of kittens.

Anything to grab attention.

Gail remembers.

"If I wanted him to pay attention to me, I'd just climb on his knee and start smoking his cigarette." (To this day, she's a non-smoker.)

"He'd laugh. He'd give me real money to play with, wads of cash. I'd stuff it into my little blue plastic purse and then forget it on the lawn overnight, and in the morning it would be gone. I don't know whether he'd picked it up, or somebody else had. It never seemed to matter."

Along with cattle, Vermilion is also horse country, and during horse auctions, Clarence could get even more creative. The western bands would do their torch-and-twang numbers, the clowns would cavort and shout one-liners into the microphone, the trick ponies would dance around on their hind legs, but Gail remembers her horses.

"I loved animals, and he'd give me a pony for a present. Make a big fuss, tell me it was my horse, just mine. Then we'd be at the auction, and he'd tell somebody to bring in my pony. And he'd sell it! Sell my pony, just like that.

"He did the same thing to Mom with her palominos. He'd give her one for a present, make a big deal of it, then he'd turn around and sell it without even asking.

"The difference was, she never really wanted the horses in the first place."

Clarence Lovig's ongoing battle with alcohol wasn't that unusual in the auction mart culture of the western prairies. Some folks even called it an occupational hazard. Some folks still do.

When a rancher made a big sale, he felt good about it. In a business where there are probably too few successes, he needed to celebrate, kick up his heels a bit. So the auctioneer would buy him a drink or two, and maybe they'd even kill the bottle. For the rancher, it might be once a year. For the auctioneer who owned the business, there'd be another sale day next week, or even tomorrow. Another sale, another bottle.

Clarence was running two auction marts, and between sales, he was hitting the road to buy cattle all over central Alberta. The drinking had become routine.

Close the deal, open the bottle.

Jean saw it happening, and she grew increasingly desperate.

"He was a man who'd see a hole right in front of him, and jump in anyway. There was drinking every night, and he'd started gambling. He'd bring his drunken friends home and expect me to cook steaks for everybody.

"It got so bad that many nights Clarence never came home at all," she says, memories flooding back, voice changing just a shade.

"I don't know which was worse."

Even as her marriage continued to crumble, Jean was determined to cobble together some sort of normal life for her children. When summer holidays rolled around, the two older boys, Lyall and Brian, both had jobs. They'd spend the summer working on the farm for their grandfather. The two youngest, Grant and Gail, asked if they could go camping. Jean packed up the car and headed south, into the Drumheller Badlands.

There was something about the strange, contorted landscape that Jean found comforting, almost spiritual. There, with the constant uncertainty of Clarence's wild alcoholic moods temporarily out of the picture, she was at peace. She could relax for a moment, watch her kids scramble around the sandstone hoodoos and give her tired brain a rest. They could camp for free, and there was a swimming pool in the campground that cost them nothing.

She remembers the smallest detail from that first trip.

"Grant was interested in geology. He had a miniature pick, and a bag tied to his belt to collect rock samples, and Gail and I watched him way up high in the hoodoos, tapping away with that pick. We noticed that the sound didn't reach us until after he'd hit the rock and raised his pick again. He had a pocketful of firecrackers, and some matches, and once, when he was trying to squeeze through a narrow hole in the rock, the firecrackers began to go off! I still can't figure out how that happened."

After sundown, they'd roast hotdogs over a campfire, watch the stars come out and listen to the night sounds of a northern desert. She'd make a bed for the kids in the back seat of the car, filling in the floor space with pillows so they'd be comfortable, while she slept on the front seat.

"It wasn't so bad. Kind of cozy, really, and the kids had fun, so I had fun too."

One night during that trip, the clouds rolled in and the rain came bucketing down in sheets, as it does in this part of the country, so they headed for an old railway hotel to wait out the storm.

They were sitting in the lobby, willing the rain to stop, when a stranger who introduced himself as Charlie Hill started talking to the children. He discovered Grant's interest in petrified relics, and invited them all up to his room, where he kept his personal collection of dinosaur bones, a giant femur, ribs, bits of jawbone found during his many years of solitary rambles through the Badlands.

"You wouldn't believe the bones he pulled out from under that bed," says Jean. "He had a museum, right there in his room."

Charlie insisted that Grant should have a petrified oyster and a number of small dinosaur bones, and the youngster was thrilled with his new acquisitions.

When the rain kept pelting down, Jean decided they'd better spend the night, so she rented the cheapest room in what was already the cheapest hotel in town.

"There was only one bed, but it was a double, and we all crawled in together. I waited until the kids fell asleep, and then I slept on the floor."

The next summer they went back to the Badlands, and Grant took a friend, Barry Jackson, with him.

Barry's mother, Kay Jackson, had been one of Jean's closest friends, and the only person with whom she was ever able to share confidences regarding her problems with Clarence.

"Kay was a nurse, and she understood about alcoholism, and what it does to people, and to their families. She had a wonderful sense of humour, and we were close, but she developed cancer.

"The last months she lived, every Wednesday, I bought two roses — one for Kay, one for myself. Then I'd go to her house and we'd talk, just the two of us. If we snipped the stems properly, the roses would last almost a week.

"Kay was a brave woman, and a great friend. When she died, I missed her terribly, and her children were far too young to be without their mother."

Jean, maybe remembering Kay's bravery, stifled her fear of rattlesnakes and let Grant and Barry sleep in a pup tent, while she and Gail slept in the car.

One hot day, Grant came running back to camp, yelling that he needed the camera. They'd found a baby rattler, and Barry was up there in the hoodoos guarding it, so hurry up or it might get away.

"We still have so many good memories of those trips," she says, her face softening as the happy times run like an old movie through her mind: the trail past the little church, the ride on the four-car ferry across the river, the suspension bridge, the ghost town.

"Once during each trip, we splurged on bumper car rides. I think the tickets were about 50 cents each, maybe less.

"Thank goodness my own car stayed in good shape during those road trips. That car was a blessing."

And so the summers passed, with Jean and Clarence struggling through a relationship that was now almost too painful to be called a marriage.

Like the Vermilion Fair, the Vermilion Rodeo was part of the western rural culture that city folk admired and envied. The annual rodeo was the real thing, part of the professional circuit, and seasoned cowboys with more grit than glitz knew every Brahma bull and bucking bronc by name and reputation.

"Here comes Rocky Rockabar aboard Spitfire," the guest announcer would sing out in his Texas drawl, as the chute opened and man and horse burst into the ring, the cowboy with one hand tightly gripping what some cowboys call a suitcase handle, the other hand raised high in the air.

Then the fiddles would start, and everybody knew they had to watch closely, because this ride would be measured in seconds only.

A good cowboy could tape his broken ribs and his blistered palms, kill the pain with a swig of rye, and wrestle a steer to the ground with his bare hands. If you sat in the front row, choking on dust, you could hear that cowboy groan.

By sundown, Bucky Swan and his western band would be playing, the liquor would be flowing, and for Clarence and his friends, it was party time again.

One of his favourite drinking companions was a rodeo clown named Buddy Heaton, who owned a trick buffalo. There is every possibility that the buffalo had more sense than Buddy, who was, by nature, a hard-drinking brawler.

Like Clarence, Buddy had a kind of fatal charm, and when he was sober, the Lovig kids enjoyed having a real, live clown for a friend. It gave them a certain celebrity-by-association. Buddy wasn't just fun, he was hilarious, as all good clowns are, and he made them laugh. But when he was drunk, things got pretty crazy.

"During the rodeo, when Buddy was in town, no day was complete without a fight," Grant recalls. "There'd be blood all over the place."

The Brahma bulls are also part of the rodeo culture. Huge, powerful, temperamental animals with names like Terminator and Sizzler, they earn their dinner by putting on a show, snorting, stomping, bucking. Now and then, when some hapless cowboy falls the wrong way, or the bull is friskier than usual, the clown can't distract him fast enough, at least not before bones are broken and brains are scrambled.

Gail was scared of the bulls. Her older brother, Lyall, remembers why.

"One day Dad was drunk, and he was teasing a huge Brahma bull named Tiger. He teased the bulls a lot, and they'd get mad. They were massive animals, very strong. Tiger darned near broke through the fence. He could have killed Dad, if he'd wanted to."

Gail, who hung out with her dad whenever possible, had seen many such moments.

If the rodeo gave Clarence one excuse to drink, Christmas gave him another.

In the early days of the auction mart, Clarence and Jean always had a big staff Christmas party, with Bucky Swan and the band playing up a storm in one corner, a full open bar in the other, Clarence being the genial host and Jean's good food in every room. By this time, she was developing a sideline as a part-time caterer, cooking for other people's parties as well as her own, and she was earning a reputation for her generous hospitality. By doing her baking ahead of time and freezing as many dishes as possible, she could handle one or two events for other people, and still load her own table with Christmas goodies for Clarence's big night.

For those parties, the kids were allowed to stay up as long as they wanted.

"It could have been so good," Grant muses, remembering how much fun it was to hang out with the adults even though you were just a squirt of a kid and likely should have been in bed hours ago.

"They could have been such a team, Mom and Dad. Her talent, his personality, and their combined business sense.

"We all loved our Dad," he says, thoughtfully. "But none of us loved the drunk."

"I think I could have coped with it if only he'd done one or the other — stayed drunk, or stayed sober," Jean says, reflecting on the wild swings in temperament, the crazy contrasts in his behaviour.

"It was the uncertainty that was so awful. Never knowing whether he'd come home happy, or come home and start hitting me … or not come home at all."

Too soon the happy house parties ended, and Christmas, the season she'd always loved so much, became the loneliest time of the year.

On one memorable Christmas Eve, while her friends' husbands were home with their families, Clarence had gone out drinking.

It got late, and she waited, leaving the Christmas lights on, hoping he'd come home just a bit sober. For hours she listened for the crunch of his boots in the snow, for his voice in the hallway.

Questions tumbled around in her brain. Where was he? Had he been in a car accident? What could have happened to keep him away all night on Christmas Eve?

Eventually, when it was nearer morning than night, she heard him stagger in. Thank God, he was alive. But when the children got up to see if Santa had come, Clarence couldn't get out of bed.

"He said he had the flu," she recalls. "He'd always say he had the flu when he had a hangover."

Clarence's repeated bouts of flu were among the little white lies Jean had begun telling her family, the face-saving excuses that might explain his increasingly odd behaviour.

"I had to do Christmas for the kids, so I got up and made a big fuss over the presents, and hoped they didn't notice anything was wrong with their dad. We drove to my parents' farm near Ardrossan for Christmas dinner, and we all pretended everything was all right.

Jean was getting good at pretending.

"I didn't tell anybody about the mess I was in. Not my parents, not my sister, not my friends. I was too embarrassed," she says, echoing words that are sadly familiar to people with alcoholic spouses.

"I was too ashamed.

"Mom and Dad never knew about his drinking," she says, and then she repeats it, as though she's no longer as convinced as she once was.

"Really, they didn't. They just didn't realize."

And if they did, they never said so.

Family portrait, with Christmas tree: Clarence is seated, with two serious-looking children beside him and one on each knee. Nobody smiles. Jean, perched nervously on the arm of the chair as if ready for flight, is looking at Clarence. Her expression is wary.

It was in Vermilion that Clarence built a new home for Jean, her dream home, with a kitchen that was the envy of her friends. She went back to work at the auction mart, running the office and coffee shop. She was also baking all the pies and making all the hamburger patties from scratch.

By 1962, she had saved enough profit from the coffee shop to buy herself a car: a brand new Chevrolet Biscayne.

But she was working too hard, worrying too much, keeping the books, trying to collect bad debts while the money Clarence made ran through his fingers like water.

One late night, exhausted mentally and physically, she headed back to Vermilion from Vegreville, where she was working one day a week. She fell asleep at the wheel of her car. The powerful Chevy crossed the road, went into a ditch and piled into some boulders.

Jean was terrified: if she had died in the accident, what would become of her children?

Outsiders who didn't belong to the tightly knit community of Vermilion might have thought the Lovigs were a model couple, but within the walls of her handsome ranch-style home, Jean's family was in chaos, and the local gossip mill was grinding busily.

She remembers watching Clarence lose an average year's salary in a single night, and it wasn't long before most of the town knew he'd added a serious gambling habit to his drinking.

During one drunken poker session in her kitchen, with Clarence losing heavily and his language toward her growing more insulting by the minute, her frustration boiled over. She took a dozen eggs out of the fridge and headed for the drunken rabble around her kitchen table.

"Leave my house! Get out, unless you want these eggs all over your cards," she yelled.

They left.

Not for the first time, Jean cried herself to sleep.

But there was worse to come. Gail remembers a particularly painful evening with her father arriving outside their house with his current girlfriend in the car, and her mother, totally humiliated and close to tears, picking up a rock and threatening to throw it through the car window.

They all remember the time Jean rented out their master bedroom when the local motel was overbooked. The bedroom had an attached bath, and Jean planned to sleep in the spare room, give the guest his breakfast the next morning, and pocket some badly needed cash.

"Somehow, Dad found out, and he came roaring home," Gail recalls. "He was threatening to kill the poor guy who'd rented the room."

This grown-up daughter laughs, nervously, but there was nothing funny about it. Not one thing, and she remembers every detail like it was yesterday.

"I remember watching Dad's fist come through the glass in the door. I remember the blood running down his arm, and my brother Brian holding him up against the house, yelling at him to behave, or he'd punch him. And of course, the police coming."

August 2005. They can laugh about it now, and they do, all four children-as-adults, gathered around the dining room table with their mother in her Edmonton condo. So many miles and years have come between the past and the present, maybe it's finally possible to see some humour in what happened to them. Like people who got in the way of a drive-by shooting and somehow survived, they laugh because it was all faintly bizarre and, truth be told, if they didn't laugh they'd probably cry, even now.

Only other survivors understand such dark humour.

At school in Vermilion, Lyall hears the gossip, or most of it.

"I can't look anybody in the eye," he accuses his father. "You owe everybody in town."

Meanwhile, Clarence seemed to take some perverse pleasure in humiliating Jean in public.

"He'd take me to a party, and leave me standing alone at the door. Then he'd ask another woman to dance. It seemed that everybody in town was talking about us."

Clarence fuelled the gossip by adding his own tidbits, insisting that Jean hadn't been home all weekend.

"It wasn't me," she protests. "I never left."

It hurt when he'd stay away all night, but the uncertainty was even worse. When he finally packed his clothes and moved out, it was almost a relief.

"He was the one that kept running out on us," she points out. "I was always there for the children."

The drinking was expensive, and so was the gambling. Clarence needed money, and even when he wasn't living there, he'd come sneaking back to the house after Jean had left for work, so he could take something to sell, anything at all, from frozen steaks to the lawn mower.

"Two of our neighbours were kind enough to keep the grass cut. They knew where the lawn mower had gone."

On one memorable morning, Jean discovered that her milk cow had gone missing.

Desperate for cash, Clarence had sold the cow.

Over several years, Jean's husband became increasingly violent, and during his binges it was she who took the brunt of his temper.

Once again, Gail remembers.

"One night when Grant and I were asleep, there was a fight, and it woke us up. Dad was hitting Mom. I remember Grant waking up and saying, 'Let's throw our toys at him.' So there we were in our pyjamas, two little kids pitching toys at our dad to distract him, so he'd stop hitting our mom.

"Grant doesn't remember the incident. He was a sensitive kid, he always blocked out the worst stuff. But I remember it all. I remember how everybody looked, I even remember what they were wearing."

Clarence got sicker, and developed delirium tremens. Violent with Jean, terrified of his own demons, he was hospitalized more than once, and was put in restraints. He ended up in an Edmonton psychiatric hospital.

For Jean, the humiliation and sadness of seeing Clarence in a straitjacket, and the fear of what he'd do when he got out, was a personal nightmare that played over and over again.

"They shot him full of enough drugs to down a horse, and still he fought. He'd be shaking so bad, he couldn't hold a glass. I'd have to hold it for him, hold the straw in his mouth ..."

Then would come the pleading, the professions of love, the promises to clean up his act once and for all. Each time, Jean would rush to his side, and she'd try again, hoping to nurse him back to health, hoping this time the promises meant something.

She lost track of broken promises.

Grant still wonders how his mother survived.

"It was psychological and physical warfare," he says. "Apart from everything else, he completely destroyed her self-esteem."

One ordinary day in 1965, Clarence walked out for good. Without a good-bye, he was gone, and the sheriff arrived to padlock the auction mart and officially inform Jean that she and her two younger kids would have one month to make other living arrangements. The mortgage company had foreclosed, and they would be evicted from their house.

"Our power was going to be cut off. I asked if they could wait one more day, and they agreed."

With one day's grace, she considered her options, but they weren't good.

"The catering wasn't enough to support us. I had no money, and no place to live. I could not, would not, ask my parents for help."

The two older boys would manage, somehow, and by this time she had almost no control over them in any case. Lyall was planning to go to university in Montana. Brian wanted to quit school and become an auctioneer.

It was the two younger ones who needed her the most. Jean packed them up and headed for Edmonton, where she still had some small equity in the house she'd made Clarence sign over to her when they moved to Vermilion.

Her marriage was over, her kids were suffering, and her future was a gaping void.

Depressed and more desperate than she'd ever felt before, Jean was headed across Edmonton's High Level Bridge in her car when suddenly she had a terrifying thought: what would happen if she just walked across the bridge and decided to jump? She wouldn't have been the first to drown her sorrows in the muddy swirl of the North Saskatchewan River.

"I decided I wouldn't be walking over that bridge for awhile," she says, with careful understatement. "I had kids to raise."

But the kids weren't happy. Jean had found a job, but Gail was skipping school and having nightmares. Some nights she'd wake up screaming.

"One night I thought I heard her screaming and I ran in, but it wasn't Gail. It was the man downstairs in the basement suite beating his wife, and *she* was screaming. It terrified all of us."

Jean took immediate action. She evicted the wife-beater and helped the woman move, hoping the husband wouldn't find out where she'd gone.

When the incident was settled, Jean knew it was time to swallow whatever pride she had left, and look after her children. She quit her job, applied for welfare, and got it.

▼ Amy and Arthur Locke, Jean's grandparents, 1925. They moved to Alberta from Summerside, Prince Edward Island.

▲ Edward and Ruby Elford on their honeymoon in Banff, 1922, at a favourite family-owned cabin.

▼ Jean's childhood home in Irma, circa 1928. Ed's stone wall led to his unusual basement garage.

▲ A former garage and gas station in Irma became Ed and Ruby Elford's general store.

▲ (Left to right) Aunt Alice and Grandma Lindsay.

▲ Jean in 1928, a few months old and barely able to sit by herself, already shows an independent streak and an interest in pretty flowers.

◄ Jean, in dark jumper, hosts her
   ninth birthday party for ten of
   her best friends.

Jean (left) at her backyard ➤
tea table with brother Ted
and friend Marjorie Webber.
Milla Mikkelson, a hired
girl, serves cookies.

◄ Jean at eleven, hair freshly curled,
   stands among the flowers in Ruby's
   prolific garden.

Jean at fifteen, in front ➤
of the Irma High School
where she took grades
10, 11 and 12.

▲ Irma Public School, circa 1939, with teacher Ray Martin. Jean, third row back, fourth from right.

▲ Military convoys from Camp Wainwright often drove along Irma's Main Street during the Second World War.

Jean on her front porch ➤ wearing her favourite dress, bought at her father's store.

▲ The Ink Spots. Back: Shirley Thomson (pianist), Jack Fletcher (drummer). Front: Carl Soneff (holding clarinet), Jean (holding saxophone).

◄ Clarence showing off, Jean looking nervous, before their marriage in 1946.

▲ Jean's wedding cake at their small reception.

▲ Clarence, polishing his beloved car before selling it to buy wedding rings.

▲ Ostad's Garage, where Clarence worked, and Jean managed to pass by twice a day.

Photo: McDermid Studios Ltd.

◄ The Lovig wedding
portrait, taken one year
after their marriage, when
they could afford it.

▲ Clarence, in his
official Vermilion
Auction Mart jacket.

▲ Taking care of business in
the Vermilion auction ring;
Clarence at the microphone.

◄ Clarence (holding baby Grant), Lyall, Jean and Brian.

▲ Baby Lyall racing toward his first birthday cake.

▲ Heading for the Saskatoon Exhibition.

▲ Grandpa Ed Elford with Brian (seated) and Lyall.

◄ Family portrait: Gail (1), Grant (4), Brian (8) and Lyall (11).

◄ Christmas, 1957: Lyall, Gail, Clarence, Brian, Grant and Jean, at the Elford house.

Christmas, 1960: ➤ Stress beginning to show in both adults.

◄ Christmas, 1965: Brian, Lyall, Gail, Jean, Grant. Clarence is no longer in the picture.

Meanwhile, Grant was quietly miserable.

When Jean asked what his problem was, he told her bluntly that he wanted to go home, to Vermilion.

So Jean put the house up for sale and once again loaded her car, with what were by now her greatly reduced worldly possessions, and headed back.

Life was never simple for Jean in those days, and it was almost prophetic that the family cat, a big black-and-white stray whose name was Mother Cat, would do her part. She chose to give birth to a litter of handsome kittens during the trip home.

"She was well named," says Grant. "Mother Cat was the matriarch of all cats, tough, fiercely protective, the terror of the local dog population."

No doubt feeling a common bond with the new mother, and having nowhere else to go, Jean settled her little family, Grant, Gail, cat, kittens and all, into a tent beside the Vermilion River.

It was the beginning of July, school was out, and the summer lay ahead. If we're going to be homeless, she thought, this is the best possible season. The long, warm days were in their favour, and she was oddly thankful for small mercies. Jean made beds on the tent floor, and they lived out of the trunk of her car. She cooked the simplest possible meals on the wood stove in the picnic shelter, and tried to make it seem like fun, as though they were just having a holiday at the lake, albeit somewhat longer than usual.

The worst time was when it rained and their beds got soaked.

"The kids had lots of sleepovers with friends, and one very kind family took us in for short periods," she says. "But you can't impose."

As the weeks passed, Jean operated in a kind of fog, and spent sleepless nights worrying. How could this have happened to her once-perfect world? More importantly, how could she rescue her family from this mess?

Summer waned and as the days grew shorter, nights in the tent began to take on a decided chill. A friend in town intervened.

"Jean, you can't live in that tent," he insisted. "Winter's coming."

He had a cabin by the water, and she could use it, rent-free. Gratefully, Jean moved kids and cats into the cottage. But, not unlike the tent, the cottage was also heat-free, and according to Gail, it was infested with moths.

"I don't remember the moths," says Jean. "I was grateful for a roof over our heads."

September 2004. In Jean's comfortable kitchen, the visiting goes on, and the smell of coffee tells the assembled friends that a fresh pot is brewing.

Behind the table where the women are seated, the big bay window overlooks the valley. From the deck of this house, if she looks west, Jean can almost see the park where she once pitched her tent like some latter-day nomad, made beds on the ground for her children, and cooked their meals in the picnic shelter.

Jean: "It wasn't too bad, except when it rained."

Gail: "We always knew we had a home with Mom, no matter what. We just knew."

Jean is, and always has been, one hundred per cent mother, and her devotion to her children has never wavered. No matter what happened to her marriage, and no matter how wounded she felt by Clarence's behaviour, the kids came first.

As the boys were growing up, she tried to be both mother and father, whether that meant driving Lyall to a farmer's field before dawn so he could go duck hunting when he was still too young to drive himself, or buying firecrackers in Edmonton for Grant so he could resell them in Vermilion at a profit.

"She bought me my first model rocket," Grant remembers. "She'd get up early with me to watch the launches from Cape Kennedy."

When Brian was in a car accident that mangled his front teeth and pushed them into his jaw, the child didn't shed a tear until Jean came flying into the room and he knew it was safe to cry.

Gail remembers the birthday parties, each of them in great detail.

In years when Jean could hardly scare up grocery money, there'd be the party, the presents, the big chiffon cake with pink icing, and the coins hidden inside.

"She knew what kids wanted, and how kids felt. It was important to her that we were happy, and carefree, as children should be," Gail recalls.

"One birthday she made us all banana splits. Real ones, with maraschino cherries, chocolate sauce and whipped cream. Nobody else's mother did that. Just mine."

The Vermilion Hotel sits on a side street, half a block off Main. It's a seedy looking place, even today, with a bar aptly named The Zoo. Attached to it is a low-slung structure once known as the Rio Cafe, and a third section, then called the Vermilion Block, that was an apartment house. In later years, the Vermilion Block would burn down, but in the mid '60s it became a temporary roof over the heads of Jean and her two youngest children.

With her marriage in tatters, Jean decided to put her business skills on the market. She talked a local banker into a $1,000 small business loan as a down payment, and bought the Rio Cafe. Then she moved the kids into rooms in the adjoining apartment block and hired more staff, planning to be home each afternoon as soon as school was out, or maybe before. But it didn't work that way.

"She was at work from six a.m. to after ten o'clock," Gail remembers. "We hardly saw our Mom."

And once again, the kids were miserable.

"I hated that place so much," Grant recalls. "I stayed away as much as possible."

Across the street was the Boston Confectionary Store, owned by the Wong family, and it became Grant's refuge. Mei Wong was in Grant's class at school, and although they weren't close friends, they certainly knew each other. His father didn't seem to mind Grant being around his store.

"I'd hang out in the Boston Confectionary until closing time, just to keep from going home. One day I actually found a drunk stuffed into a baby carriage at the bottom of the stairs."

Jean wasn't happy either.

"I had to leave for work before they got up. I had no free time. If the cook was sick, or the dishwasher quit, I had to be there. I knew the kids were suffering. Gail was going to school without her hair combed."

Then the house in Edmonton sold, and Jean was able to put a down payment on a house in Vermilion. It wasn't grand, but it was comfortable, and infinitely better than their brief stint in the apartment.

Jean's marriage to Clarence Lovig had ended in divorce in 1966, but no matter how conflicted their lives together had been, he was the man she had always loved, the father of her children.

"We had a lot of history together," she says, remembering the good times.

After the divorce was final, they stayed in contact, even after he'd remarried and they became, in Jean's words, "almost friendly."

Without the constant worry and humiliation, Jean's life and that of her children improved dramatically. She even began dating, although the men Gail remembers had a pretty tough time romancing a woman like Jean.

"I always told them I didn't entertain men in my home, and I meant it."

While there wasn't exactly an army of eligible men knocking at the door, Jean was an attractive woman, and Gail remembers a modest parade of suitors, some of them definitely more suitable than others.

"They tried hard," Gail says, remembering how she and Grant dealt with them.

"They'd bring her chocolates, and we'd eat them. They'd bring her flowers, and we'd giggle. She'd say 'I'll go out with you, but my kids will have to come too.'

"So we'd all go to the drive-in, and watch *Creature from the Black Lagoon,* or *The Mummy's Revenge,* and Mom's date would buy us popcorn. One guy had a flat tire on the way home, and we locked all the doors while he was out there in the dark, fixing it. Some of the guys were pretty funny, and I don't think she took any of them seriously."

Although Clarence never came out of his alcoholic tailspin, during the last few years of his life he managed to have periods when he was sober. During those times, he made an attempt to repair the relationship with his children, and all four of them were able to spend some positive time with their father. In retrospect, Jean is grateful for that.

"He'd even phone me," she recalls. "We'd talk."

Sadly, Clarence's attempts at reform were a classic example of too little, too late.

At fifty-nine, Jean's first love, the best dancer in the world, suffered a heart attack and died. He was broke, and alone.

Gail Lovig: "In all those years, she never spoke badly of Dad, not to us. She never stopped loving him, either. She wanted that other Clarence, the one she knew was there somewhere inside him, but it just didn't happen."

There had been one bright note in the whole Rio Cafe fiasco. His name was Larry Paré, and he was an electrician, a big, good-looking guy with dark hair and an easy laugh. When Jean took over, he became a regular at the Rio.

"At first he just came for pie and coffee, but he did seem to be there a lot," Jean remembers. "He often came for lunch with his son. He said he loved my apple pie."

Larry was a single father and Jean was now a single mother. It gave them a common bond, something to talk about. When Jean announced that after six months as owner she'd had enough of cafe life — she was selling the Rio — he offered her a deal: if he and his son could eat their noon meal at Jean's house, he'd pay all her grocery bills.

She took him up on it.

Larry was different than the other men she'd met after Clarence left, and Jean enjoyed his company. With him she felt safe. Here was a man she could count on, one who actually wanted to look after her.

In 1968, Larry Paré and Jean Lovig were married by a United Church minister in Wainwright. When Gail asked if she could come to the wedding, Jean said no.

"You weren't at my first wedding, and I see no reason why you should be at this one."

The Lovigs and the Parés became a blended family. Larry didn't try to be a father to the Lovig kids, and Jean didn't try to mother his children. It was a wise policy, and they all got along.

"Mom has been close to his three kids," says Grant. "She still is. She has organized family trips to places like Nashville, Disneyland, Hawaii, with herself and Larry, all the kids and all their spouses. She has worked hard to make us all feel included, like we're one big family."

September 2004. Jean, in her office at Company's Coming, leafs through a pamphlet from Alcoholics Anonymous.

"When I was going through all that trouble with Clarence, I'd heard of AA, but I didn't really know what they were, or how to contact them. There was no Al-Anon in those days, at least not in Vermilion. No help for families of alcoholics, no safe places ... " and for reasons that might be understood only by other women in her position, she'd been too ashamed to tell anybody what she was going through.

"I don't know why that was. I guess if you have an alcoholic husband, or wife, you might understand how I felt, but still not know why you or I would try to hide it."

She sits bolt upright in her chair, her back not touching the cushions.

"I don't like what happened to us," she says.

"I still hate to think of what it did to me, how it changed me. I got so angry. I still get angry, when I remember.

"Not with my kids — never with my kids — but with Clarence, for all the pain, for how he hurt me, for what his drinking did to all of us ..."

Strangely, to this day, Jean can't help but wonder if she was somehow the cause of his problems.

Intellectually, she knows that Clarence's alcoholism was a disease, and it had nothing to do with her. But still, there's that inkling of doubt: what could she have done differently?

"His drinking brought out the worst in me. I did lots of things I probably shouldn't have done. I fought back when I could, and I talked back."

Even now, the unreasonable guilt is there in the back of her mind, the nagging feeling that maybe, somehow, in some way, she was responsible.

"Maybe he wouldn't have hit me if I'd been quiet? I don't know. I've wondered about that.

"I was lonely, and I went to a few parties that I wish I hadn't. I soon found out they didn't help the loneliness ..."

She pauses, searching for some redemptive moment here, something of value she might rescue from those troubled years.

"The only good that might come of all those bad times would be if I could help just one other person, keep one person from going through what we went through."

So what would she tell them, if she could, these phantom women she knows are out there, scared and silent, hiding from the truth?

"I'd say this: If he hasn't been home all week, if he's lying to you, if he's blaming you for his problems, if he's suspicious of you, if he's blacking out, if you can't do anything right no matter how hard you try, if he's hiding liquor around the house, if he hits you even once ... get help.

"Don't wait. Ask for help right now. Today," she says.

"Phone Alcoholics Anonymous. Phone Al-Anon. Tell somebody you trust."

FOUR

THE MAIN THING
An accidental caterer

During the last years of her marriage, Jean had worried constantly about her financial future. Knowing that her relationship with Clarence had become a personal and financial liability, she spent countless hours wondering what lay ahead for herself and her children.

One lucky day back in 1963, just when she needed it most, fate stepped in with an opportunity for Jean. It was one of those odd accidents of time and place, and although she couldn't have known it at the time, eventually that incident would redefine her life.

A friend had come into the auction mart office and happened to mention that he needed help with a project — the 50th anniversary reunion for the Vermilion Agricultural College. He needed a caterer, desperately, and hadn't been able to find anyone, anywhere, that was willing to take on the job.

"I'll do it," Jean said.

The man was so relieved he almost did handstands right there in the office.

Only then did she ask the question she probably should have asked first.

"How many people?"

"Maybe a thousand. Probably more."

"Excuse me?"

"More than a thousand. We'd be safe to say twelve hundred."

It was a jaw-dropping statement, and she had no idea why she'd blithely volunteered to take on a job that would have given a professional caterer a headache. The friend took her up on it before she could change her mind and Jean had a new profession: accidental caterer.

"I thought it was one shot, one time," she says. "I had no intention of doing it more than once."

But a deal's a deal. Just do it, her Dad had always told her, so Jean started making lists.

"I still make lists," she says. "Before a party or a dinner, even if it's just for the family, I write down every single task that has to be done. Then I feel organized, and it gives me confidence."

With no catering experience, no commercial kitchen or proper equipment, she had roughly thirty days to whip her project into shape and get it launched. Thirty days to figure out how she was going to cook and serve a dinner for the proverbial small army of more than 1,000 people.

The menu itself was simple enough. They wanted a cold plate, and that was something to be thankful for. She wasn't about to try any gourmet tricks — there'd be no shrimp cocktails or crêpes Suzette — and she wisely stuck to a plan that was almost an extended picnic, the sort of meal she'd made dozens of times for Sundays at the lake. It had been Ruby's menu too, back in the days of the swimming hole at the Battle River, when life had been a lot simpler.

Turkey; ham; three or four salads: green, potato and jellied. You couldn't have a prairie party without at least one jellied salad. "They make the table look so pretty," she says.

Buns, of course, and for dessert, ice cream. She'd buy Dixie Cups. They'd save on labour, and by using enough dry ice she could keep the ice cream from melting and running all over the place.

It was a good start, but how much of everything would she need? God forbid she should run short, or worse, run out. In Vermilion, that would finish a caterer faster than a speeding bullet, and although it might be the only catering job she ever got, she wasn't about to blow it. Prairie parties were noted for tables so full they groaned, and she could not skimp on anything. It was a policy that she would maintain throughout her career.

"Have you ever been to a catered party where they ran out of food?"

It's a rhetorical question, and she gets a chuckle out of remembering those few occasions she's attended as a guest, when the unfortunate caterer has done just that, and had some unhappy customers staring at empty platters.

"I can't figure out why that happens," she says. "All they have to do is count."

Counting was critical. The party would take some canny figuring, so Jean sharpened her pencil and went to work.

For her first effort, she intended to start with 20 turkeys, nice big ones, about 25 pounds each, 500 pounds altogether, and she'd get the local baker, Nick

Klemantovich, to roast them in his bread ovens. After all, she'd be buying at least 120 dozen of his dinner buns, and that should earn a few brownie points where the oven was concerned.

Then, 250 pounds of ham. Boneless picnics, pre-baked, so she wouldn't have to worry about it at the last minute.

Next, the essential potato salad: potatoes, eggs, green onion, radishes, her homemade mustard-spiked dressing, Ruby's own recipe.

"Of course the dressing would be slightly different for each woman, but I always used my mother's recipe. It was a cooked dressing, done in a double boiler, with flour, mustard, vinegar, sugar and an egg. It's also good for devilled eggs."

When potato salads were on the menu, many prairie cooks used basically the same recipe, but the relative amounts of mustard and vinegar they used in the dressing made the difference between a bland salad and what some people called a real plate-licker.

"I knew a lot of women with big gardens," Jean said. "They all had canners, those big blue enamel pots that held seven quart sealers each."

If she enlisted ten friends, and asked each one to cook a canner full of potatoes, at roughly 32 pounds per canner, she'd have a good start on 320 pounds of potato salad. With that, the third vital ingredient in any successful prairie banquet, after turkey and ham — the potato salad — would be covered.

For her green salad, she decided to buy head lettuce, because it was sturdier than leaf lettuce from the garden. Seventy-five extra-large, extra-firm heads of iceberg lettuce should be enough. Jellied salads were certain hits at community suppers, so she'd borrow the top shelf in five fridges for two days, and make 15 gallons each of two of her favourite jellied salads: golden glow, with lemon Jell-O and grated carrots, and colleen, based on lime Jell-O and cottage cheese.

After that, it got easier. Sweet pickles, 5 gallons; dill pickles, 5 gallons. She'd need a gallon of mustard for the ham, 30 pounds of butter for the buns. Plan for 2,000 cups of coffee, 20 quarts of cream, 20 pounds of sugar cubes, and 1,500 Dixie Cups for dessert. Better to have a few dozen over than to be short by one.

The weeks flew, and Jean worried. What if there wasn't enough food? Just to be certain it wouldn't happen, she made a last-minute addition to the menu: baked beans. They were a staple at picnics, served cold. She had no time to bake them from scratch, so she added 168 large cans of baked beans with molasses and tomato sauce to her grocery list.

Today, Jean wonders where all those lists went, and wishes she had kept them.

"I suppose I was in a hurry, and they just got thrown away. Later, I started keeping everything — grocery lists, menus, and I'd write comments about what was left over and what we needed more of."

September 2004. In her Edmonton office, the woman whose books outsell almost everything but the dictionary smiles about that first job, still wondering how she ever scared up the nerve to try.

The night before the big event, the phone kept ringing, friends kept stopping by to offer help, and by midnight, Jean had developed a major case of stage fright.

"I didn't sleep at all that night."

What if there wasn't enough food? People got cranky over things like that. (No, the baked beans would take up any slack.)

What if the turkeys were half raw? Prairie folks like their steaks rare and their turkey falling off the bone. (No, the baker would never let that happen, he liked his turkey well done too.)

What if … What if … until sunrise.

Early in the morning she packed the Chevy to the roof and made the first of many trips to the college, where a large machine shop called the Mechanic's Building had been designated as the only spot big enough to hold such a crowd.

Thank goodness for paper plates, it kept the weight down for the Chevy, and there wouldn't be many dishes to wash.

By noon, the big shop was beginning to look like a restaurant, or at the very least, a banquet hall.

Late in the afternoon, the women started arriving with food. She had finally let them assemble the potato salads at home, using their own dressing, but cautioning them all to add it no more than one hour ahead of time.

"You can't be too careful with potato salad," she says firmly. "The last thing I needed was a lot of people getting stomach aches from eating my potato salad."

She'd invested in some Rubbermaid tubs, each one laundry-sized, big enough to hold 100 servings of salad. When it was time to toss them, she grated in some red cabbage for colour, added green onions from the garden and threw in some dried onion for good measure. The lettuce went in last, seven heads per tub, and she made a good vinaigrette dressing to add at the last minute.

The baker arrived with his truck full of buns and well-done turkeys. Rapidly, decisively, she parcelled out the jobs: two people to carve turkeys, one to carve ham, all carving to be done in the kitchen.

"I didn't want any carving done at the buffet table, because it takes too long. There's nothing more frustrating than having to wait in the food line while somebody stands there discussing how big a slice they want, and making up his mind over light meat or dark. We carved in the kitchen, and then all they had to do was stick a fork in the piece they wanted."

Other kitchen helpers were assigned the task of keeping the bowls filled and refilled. Once that was done, she could tick off another item on her lengthy to-do list, and her troops were finally ready for battle.

The party took off, with a dozen food lines moving at once. Vermilion had never seen anything like it. Neither had Jean, but it worked.

"I often wonder why caterers don't use more than two food lines," she muses. "It's just so much faster if you have four tables and eight lines, or six tables and twelve lines. It's the same amount of food in the end, and everybody gets to sit down and eat at almost the same time. I always feel so sorry for those poor people at the last table called to the buffet, who don't even get to eat their salad until everybody else is almost ready for dessert."

When Jean's first big catering job was almost over, and she and her friends could finally heave a sigh of relief and think about cleaning up the leftovers, her daughter, Gail, came running into the hall with a soft drink in a glass bottle.

"I think Clarence had dropped her off, so she could see us in action at this big catering job. Clarence likely wanted to have a look too. He was kind of proud of me, I think. Especially at first."

For some reason, Gail tripped and fell. The bottle broke, gashing her hand so badly that Jean had to leave the party and rush her daughter to the hospital.

"I remember all the blood, and Mom wrapping a blue checked dishtowel around my arm," Gail says, wriggling her left hand in the air.

All things considered, it was a fairly typical day in Jean's ongoing crisis-management lifestyle.

"I don't know how we did it," she says, reflecting back on a catering job that would have given an experienced caterer a nervous breakdown, considering the circumstances.

"Everybody showed up, and we just figured it out."

She charged $1.25 a plate.

Vermilion's first and only professional catering business was off and running. Nobody was more surprised than Jean Lovig.

Jean, with camera in hand, is taking pictures of her tables, set for company. "There's a proper way to set a table," she says. "This is how I want it to look."

Of all the catering she would do in the next eighteen years, Jean's perennial favourites were the local high school graduation banquets, with the boys all spit-and-polished, the girls self-consciously gorgeous, the parents looking proud, and everybody using their best manners.

One year as the celebrations got rolling and Jean and her crew were getting ready to serve the banquet, it became apparent that they were running short of certain essentials.

"We didn't have enough plates, or cutlery, or glasses. We were running out of tomato juice. It didn't make sense," said Jean, the chronic over-supplier at every event. Within minutes, she had waylaid an organizer and solved the mystery.

"When the committee counted the numbers, they'd forgotten to include the grads, and there were eighty-eight of them!"

Jean knew she wasn't at fault, and she didn't want any prospective customers thinking she was. She suggested in a firm and compelling tone that an announcement should be made to explain what had happened.

Meanwhile, she barrelled around town in the trusty Chevy, gathering up supplies for an extra eighty-eight by now exceedingly hungry graduates.

"It wasn't really a problem, because I always kept extra supplies at home for emergencies. You never know when you'll need an extra few gallons of tomato juice."

As her skills improved and her business grew, Jean was soon the one to call for any catered meal, whether it was a major festivity like a wedding, or something small, like a Rotary meeting. Fifteen or fifteen hundred, there was nothing she wouldn't tackle.

She also had a few near misses.

Once, while she was carrying a 100-cup urn of hot coffee, a handle broke.

"Have you any idea how much coffee that is? It's a flood!"

After that, she had a local carpenter design and build special carts to move heavy items like full pots and coffee urns.

It took awhile to assemble the tools of her trade, but gradually Jean invested in bigger and better equipment, larger cooking pots, roasters, long-handled potato mashers.

Then she had a second-hand commercial fridge and another stove moved into the garage to give her more cooking possibilities. She also learned to stow certain essential items in a tackle box, and carry it with her at all times: her favourite knives, serving spoons, beer openers, pickle forks, sugar tongs, all the gadgets and gizmos that were critical to the smooth running of a catered meal, in places often ill-equipped to have them.

September 2004. The women around the table have heard these stories before, and they smile and nod, and remember. They all watched the growth of the catering enterprise, sometimes as guests, sometimes as helpers.

The coffee pot comes around again, and Jean serves lemon squares while they have a group chuckle over the only time she accidentally double-booked an event. They remember, because it was such an unusual lapse in her almost military operational skills.

On that night, at exactly six o'clock, the members of the Royal Purple Lodge were supposed to be starting dinner in the Vermilion Elks Hall, sipping their chilled glasses of tomato juice, teeth all set for roast beef. At the same time, thirty hungry people from the Goodwill Society would also be sitting down at the golf course clubhouse, and they too would be waiting for their supper.

A nightmare! What to do?

Jean got on the phone and a friend, Gudrun Baranyk, stepped up to help, as her friends so often did. Gudrun had helped cater on other occasions, and she knew the ropes.

"That's the only time I double-booked by accident," Jean reminds them, and Gudrun, a pleasant, grey-haired woman sitting at the end of the table, smiles broadly. It's something they like to reminisce about during these weekly coffee parties, now that it's all over and they never, ever have to do it again.

Still, as her business grew, it was inevitable that events would stack up on the same night, and once in awhile she'd have three parties booked in three different venues and two different towns. Friends would take over and shepherd one event through for her while she presided at another, but she always insisted on personally hauling all the food herself, starting out in the afternoon with the car (by now a Mercury Marquis with a huge trunk) heavily loaded, delivering supplies to each location. That way, she kept track of everything, checked on the table settings, and made certain that nobody ever went short of anything.

But a growing business isn't necessarily a prosperous business, and Jean found catering to be increasingly expensive, with the law of diminishing returns beginning to hit her hard.

Margaret Snelgrove, a lifelong friend, explains what happened.

"Jean was competing with free labour," she says. "In small towns, weddings and big community events are often catered by one service group or another. Mostly they're from the churches, and they donate everything. Before Jean came along, that's all we had."

If she was going to stay in business, something had to change.

"I never made money on full service," Jean said. "By that time my daughter Gail, and Grant's girlfriend, Frieda, were in high school, and they'd collect fifteen or twenty girls to serve, with one server for every twenty guests. I always paid above minimum wage, but after the girls left it was getting harder to find help, and labour costs were eating up my profits. So I lowered my prices and went buffet."

She served the first buffet banquets in Vermilion, and huge, country-style feasts they were, at $2.50 per plate.

"We always had fun," Margaret Snelgrove remembers. "At one event, we were laughing so much in the kitchen that Gail heard a guest in the dining hall say, 'They're all drunk in there.'"

Not so. Jean had rules, and although the odd cocktail made its way into the kitchen after most of the work was done and the local Rotarians were feeling generous, she wouldn't have tolerated drinking on the job.

"Sometimes they'd send drinks in at the end of an evening, but it was just a generous gesture after a good event," she says. At the time, many parties were dry, and she remembers one evening when she was catering a wedding party for a family of religious teetotallers.

"We were serving the usual fruit punch, and these two kids, the bride and groom, came into the kitchen with a mickey of vodka, and they discreetly asked me to spike the punch.

"I thought they were so cute, because they expected that drop-in-the-bucket to liven up the party considerably. In fact, it was a very good evening all the way around, though I doubt that the tiny dribble of vodka had anything to do with it."

As well as no drinking on the job, there was no smoking either, and no gum chewing while serving. Neat clothes, neat hair. Scrupulously clean fingernails.

Tables had to be properly set, so she took photographs of the correct settings and insisted her hired staff adhere to them.

She always over-delivered: if a client asked for a cold plate, Jean added a casserole; if they asked for one salad, she served at least two or three, but more often six.

"It didn't have to be elaborate, but the extras always went over well, whether it was a bowl of spiced crabapples or a tray of sliced melon."

Dessert, however, did have to be special.

"It had to require a fork. That was my rule. Cake, pie, whatever it was, it needed to look as good on the plate as it tasted going down."

By now, Jean was experimenting a bit, trying new recipes on her clientele.

One night she served Cornish game hens, and it was apparently the first time such a tiny version of a chicken had made its way onto the plates of some of her customers.

Midway through the meal, an astonished server came back to the kitchen to announce that a guest had wrapped his game hen in an impromptu doggie bag and stowed it on the floor. It was down there right now, she said, right beside his foot. Just go and look.

"I went in to see if there was something wrong," says Jean. "Sure enough, there it was on the floor.

"He said, 'I've never seen one of these little fellas before. I'm taking it home to show my wife!'"

Jean loved setting a handsome table. It was one of the pleasures of her business, and she continued to deliver more than her clients expected, whether with trays of sliced fruit and moulded jellied salads, or bowls of bean salad and coleslaw when none had been expected.

"Most buffets serve salads and buns first. Now why is that?" she wonders. "Maybe they're hoping you'll fill up on the cheap items before you get to the expensive things — the hot meat dishes."

That was not how she did things.

"I served the meat and hot dishes first, and I always served two meats. And right from that first event, we continued to carve in the kitchen, so nobody would hold up the line at a carving station, deciding whether they wanted well done or rare. Not that they'd have had a choice, because all the meat I cooked was served well-done," she says firmly. "And, it was always tender."

Having loaded and unloaded so many heavy boxes, and lugged them up and down so many flights of stairs, often at a run, Jean was in the best physical shape she'd ever been in. She felt strong and healthy. She also had a large, loyal clientele that enjoyed her food and her hospitable service so much that they were booking parties a year in advance, and happily juggling dates so Jean could fit them into her calendar. They were also telling her to choose the menu.

In the first two weeks of December, she'd routinely do two dozen Christmas parties, complete with roast turkey, baked ham and all the trimmings.

"They were big meals, and at the end, we went all-out on dessert. There was always plum pudding with sauce, mince tarts, shortbread and squares. I always included my Neapolitan squares, because of the pink icing."

Jean began scheduling baking sessions in early October, freezing puddings, tarts, cookies and a huge variety of un-iced squares. It was the only way she could have been ready for all the Christmas feasting.

As her reputation spread, so did the number of important events she was cooking for. Over the years, many political celebrities sat down to one of Jean's meals. Often when the official host would bring the guest of honour back to the kitchen to meet the caterer and say thank you for his supper, he'd find that Jean and his honourable guest were already well acquainted, whether it was the Alberta minister of education, or the deputy prime minister of Canada. Celebrities didn't faze her, not even meeting Colonel Harland Saunders of Kentucky Fried Chicken fame. In later years, when her son Brian organized a celebrity swap meet in Reno with Bob Hope as his guest speaker, Jean didn't turn a hair.

One night, while serving strawberry shortcake to former deputy prime minister Don Mazankowski, she ended up with her thumbprint in his whipped cream.

"Whoops, Don, my thumb slipped," she said breezily, grinning at the VIP, and horrifying some of his guests.

"I think they were rather shocked," she says. "So I put them out of their misery and told them I'd known Don a long time before he went into politics, when we still had the auction marts and he was a car dealer in Vegreville."

When she cooked for a homecoming where the beloved Lt.-Gov. Grant MacEwan was a guest, he shook her hand and shouted, in the booming voice of a nearly deaf man, "Those are the best baked beans I ever ate."

"They were just my doctored-up beans," she says. "I told him he must have been especially hungry that night."

The other women in the kitchen with her always had time to perch on the edge of a chair, if only briefly, and enjoy a meal and a bit of socializing, but Jean would munch on an unbuttered bun while checking the salads or slicing more meat. God forbid that she should take a minute to slap butter on that bun — she might miss some minor crisis in the dining room.

"I still eat buns without butter," she says.

The smallest event she ever catered was a meeting for ten people. The biggest (and there were several) were for 1,500, and true to her prairie roots, Jean insisted on speedy service, no matter how big the crowd.

"We got more efficient with time," she says. "At one school reunion for 1,200, we had everybody fed and watered in twenty minutes!" It was a meal they still talk about, not just because of the efficient service, but because the food was so good.

"Nick Klemantovich, the baker, had roasted the boned and rolled short hips of beef, and he also did the cabbage rolls and baked potatoes in his oven, as well as the buns. I think we had about ten buffet tables that night, and twenty food lines."

Another meal she's never forgotten was the wedding reception for her son, Grant, and Frieda Boier, his high school sweetheart.

"Larry arranged to have the beef pit-barbecued, cooking the roasts low and slow for upwards of eight hours, until the meat was so tender you could cut it with a fork."

Although she was always experimenting with different dishes for her menus, and was happy to take all reasonable requests, Jean dug in her heels when it came to barbecuing steaks.

"The Kinsmen Club used to ask for steak every time, and every time I'd say no, because the only way I cook steak is well done. So they stopped asking."

With her unassuming style and her home-cooked meals, Jean had a way of making everybody comfortable. She made the whole thing look easy, as though she just breezed in and snapped her fingers, and abracadabra, it magically appeared.

In fact, quite the opposite was true. She worried before every event.

"I always suffered a sort of stage fright before every function. What if I ran out of coffee? What if each person took one extra tablespoon of vegetables?

Would there be enough? What *if*?"

Her policy of over-supplying was so well known that people began to expect that little something extra on the side, and she devised new ways to surprise them. If it was a seniors' group, serving foursomes on bridge tables, she'd make an individual moulded salad for each table, just because it looked pretty.

One night as they packed up after a banquet, a friend who'd been helping her surveyed the mountain of leftovers and gave Jean the benefit of her opinion.

"There sits your profit," she said firmly.

"No," said Jean. "There sits my peace of mind."

FIVE

FOREIGN FLAVOURS
Eating on the road

By the time Jean was in high school, she knew she wanted to travel. When they had a career day, she gave it some thought, and showed up in her classroom with a map of the world.

"I want to go everywhere," she told her astonished mother.

"I want to see the whole world."

Ruby suggested that a career might be a good idea before all that globe-trotting got started, and if she became a teacher or a nurse, it would make a lot of sense. Or, considering all the travelling she wanted to do, why not become a flight attendant, known at the time as a stewardess?

It was a safe suggestion, Ruby felt, because in those days, you had to be a registered nurse before you could train as a flight attendant, and either way, it would be good insurance for Jean's future. She'd always be able to make a living for herself, no matter what.

But Jean had other plans. She wasn't about to invest three more years on formal education when there was an entire world out there, waiting for her.

And travel she did, though it would be many years before she had a chance to do it. It was her second husband, Larry Paré, who began travelling with her.

Jean and Larry, orchid leis around their necks and mai tais in hand, smile into the camera. This is the life.

Alberta winters are long and cold, and in January of 1970, Jean and Larry launched their first adventure on foreign soil by joining some friends for a trip to Hawaii. When the plane touched down and the doors opened, she got her first whiff of tropical air. Jean felt as though she'd fallen into paradise.

It was a time before Canadians had invaded Hawaii in such great numbers, when Honolulu bars still served every mai tai in a fresh pineapple, and a local entertainer named Don Ho was young, sober, and just beginning to build a career with his signature number, *Tiny Bubbles*.

The first time she tasted a field-cut pineapple, with juice dripping from golden, perfumed flesh, Jean was thrilled right down to her toes. Finally, she understood how pineapple is supposed to taste!

The velvety texture of a ripe papaya, its flavour some elusive thing between a peach and an exotic melon, was especially wonderful with a squeeze of fresh lime.

Guava juice reminded her of ripe wild strawberries, but again, there was a faint, elusive perfume, this time of crabapple jelly, while it's still hot and about to be ladled into jars.

After the hard, well-travelled versions of Hawaiian fruit she was used to buying in Alberta, it was like eating flowers, and she felt like a honeybee turned loose in a field of sweet clover.

Jean also loved macadamia nuts, and Kona coffee, and the local fish, especially the firm, sweet-fleshed mahi mahi. She wasn't crazy about lomi lomi salmon because she has never acquired a taste for raw fish, but she tried it and decided it was interesting.

At a local hangout called the Poi Bowl in the Ala Moana Shopping Center, she had her first taste of cooked fermented taro root, and when she declared it simply bland and pasty, an elderly Hawaiian man in the market reminded her that she probably ate mashed potatoes, and they were also bland and pasty.

She brought a bag of poi home for her regular catering clients, the local Rotary Club, and although they gingerly sampled it, there were no requests for seconds.

"Get used to it," she said, and laughed when they looked worried. To the relief of the Rotarians, she never got around to duplicating the great Hawaiian luau with kalua pig, lomi lomi salmon and poi.

Jean fell in love with the Hawaiian islands. It was a trip she and Larry would make about twenty times, and to this day she is still in touch with people she met on that first vacation in paradise.

In 1971, Jean and Larry took off for Spain. In spite of their ever-present map, they were constantly lost, hopping on and off the wrong buses, veering off into the wrong alleys, hearing the echoes of their own footsteps on the cobblestones.

The old part of Madrid was a labyrinth, and they enjoyed being lost, wandering along boulevards lined with orange trees.

"Seville oranges," she remembers. "The kind I wanted for my marmalade."

They went to Seville, and she remembers being shown a certain barber shop, and being told by an enterprising guide that it was the original business address of the original Barber of Seville, the true and certain hangout for the original Don Juan of operatic fame, but once again it was the food that she found exciting. The seafood, the outdoor cooking of a true, over-the-fire paella, the cool, crunchy soup they called gazpacho — all these impressions were committed to memory.

From southern Spain, it was a quick hop to Morocco, where she dived into the covered markets of Tangier's old casbah, and found it full of characters who looked like they'd stepped out of the Bible, all crying their wares at once, trying to sell her a bargain.

Among the black-robed women, the colours were all the more intense within the dim shops. Lemons and oranges with waxy green leaves still attached glowed like small light bulbs. Then there were the mounds of tiny dried rosebuds for making tea, the rainbow of spices whose names she was hearing for the first time, great baskets overflowing with armloads of fresh herbs, the fragrance of mint, flat-leaf parsley, roses, lavender, the taste of honey and sweet black coffee … it was magic, like something out of *The Arabian Nights*.

Not so the meat markets, which she found primitive and intimidating, with carcasses of small and large animals hanging in close, fetid alleys, flies picnicking on the meat, and a butcher in a blood-stained tunic hacking off pieces of lamb or goat as each shopper came along.

"I'll never forget the poultry. There'd be a bird of some kind, plucked and hanging by its neck, and it seemed that the butcher would cut off whatever the shopper wanted — sometimes a leg, or even just a wing — but in that market, I didn't see one person buying a whole bird."

There were fresh adventures around every corner, and though Larry was less excited than she about some of what they saw and tasted, it was wonderful to have somebody to share it with.

"We found a restaurant, and I remember that the food, some sort of couscous maybe, was delicious. From our table, we overlooked small huts where someone kept a few chickens on the roof, and it seemed very sensible. At least you'd never run out of eggs!"

On their first trip to England, Jean went out for afternoon tea and was delighted to discover, on the third tier of the cake tray, some small, yeasty pancakes called pikelets and the Scottish specialty known as baps. As always, she began salting away new recipe ideas, constantly jotting notes in anticipation of home and her own kitchen.

But the back roads of rural England were a far cry from the wide open spaces of Alberta, and the narrow lanes that wound between stone fences and tall hedgerows made her too nervous to drive, "Especially on the wrong side of the road. I had a stomach ache for three days!"

Still, there was research to be done, and she marvelled over the gas-fired pull-out grill she saw in many British kitchens, and thoroughly enjoyed the concept of the mixed grilled breakfast of sausages, bacon, tomatoes and mushrooms.

Never having approved of the French food fad that took both the fat and the fun out of eating, she wasn't any happier with the *nouvelle cuisine* trend of undercooking vegetables and serving them al dente. She and a friend, Helen Urwin, who by this time was working at Company's Coming, attended Anne Willan's Paris cooking school, La Varenne. They were amazed at the lavish use of cream, butter and eggs at a time when the French seemed to be madly backpedalling into a dietary regime that was not only devoid of all those delicious fats, but was also barely cooked.

When she discovered her new British friends still cooking their vegetables for rather a long time — some would say too long — she felt vindicated.

"I want my vegetables cooked," she says firmly. "Not mushy, but cooked. I never liked those barely warm carrots crunching in my teeth."

She loved the fish and chips wrapped in newspapers, but the much-vaunted British beef left her unimpressed, especially when she tried to order it in those cute country pubs.

"Several times, when we ordered roast beef, we found ourselves eating re-heated beef with canned potatoes. If we wanted good beef, we had to order it in a hotel dining room, and it was darned expensive.

"Coming from Alberta, I was used to the best beef in the world. I always bought a boned and rolled short hip, and oven-roasted it low and slow, with the roaster lid on, so it self-basted. I know that's completely against everything that's ever been written about how to roast beef, but my mother always did it that way, so I did too. It was always tender, and I didn't have all that mess to clean up in the oven."

In 1975, Jean and Larry booked one of the around-the-world adventures that was available for a few short years, with unlimited stopovers flying with any airline as long as they kept travelling in the same direction. They stopped in Hawaii, Fiji, New Zealand, Australia, Hong Kong, Singapore, Thailand, India and England before setting foot back in Canada. On a later trip, having received a book order from a restaurant in Singapore, she astonished the chef by showing up at the kitchen door with the book in her hand, personally delivered by the author. They also hand-delivered a case-lot order to Foyles, a huge bookstore in London.

"At that time, they told us it was the world's biggest bookstore," she recalls.

Soon they headed off to cruise the Caribbean, and in 1979 they did a second around-the-world trip, adding to their previous itinerary the Philippines, New Delhi in India and several parts of Kenya, where she was chased by a cantankerous rhino.

On her first trip to India, Jean had been shocked by the extreme poverty of Bombay, now called Mumbai. Even the food markets with their high-piled vegetables and small mountains of exotic spices and brilliantly coloured flowers failed to interest her, because of the swarms of flies that were forever landing on the produce, and the flocks of beggars that seemed to follow them everywhere. She found the tattered, begging children to be heart-rending. How could anybody ignore a three-year-old, pleading for a few rupees with tiny, grubby hands upraised?

But by their second trip to India she knew what to expect, and how to deal with it.

"I stayed away from any man sitting cross-legged on the ground with a lidded basket, because he was almost certain to have a live snake in it."

She also learned to be very selective about the beggars she gave money to, because no matter how pitiful they seemed, if she handed money to one child, he'd immediately be replaced by five others. This was especially hard for Jean, who has for many years supported a large extended family of foster children in several different countries, and believes strongly in what she calls, "being charitable to needy people."

"But when there are wild budgies flitting through the trees, and so much beauty right before your eyes, you get over the culture shock," she says. "You have to get beyond it, or you'd miss so much of what is good about India."

New Delhi was a different city, easier on her western eyes, and when she made friends with a cab driver, he took Jean and Larry home with him, to his apartment, so they could see how he lived, with his mother and his shy, pretty sister-in-law.

Indian food was a new fascination. Listening to the snap and sizzle of frying spices, watching the bakers in the street markets slap the dough onto the inside wall of a hot tandoori oven to make the soft flatbread called naan, seeing them grind the freshly toasted seeds of coriander and mustard in a mortar for their own garam masala, Jean sampled each dish tentatively, because of the heat, but she paid attention to every nuance. She knew that here she was eating history.

She has always had a sweet tooth, so she tried as many Indian desserts as she could, and developed a taste for gulab jaman and carrot halwa, and was determined to try them in her own kitchen.

Not every experiment was a success, and some of the flavours just didn't taste right to her western palate.

"Among the Indian desserts, I found that rosewater and orange flower water could easily overwhelm a dish, and make it taste like perfume. It wasn't something I enjoyed."

Home again in Vermilion, she had a head full of memories and a purse stuffed with recipes to be tested in her own kitchen: chicken curry, onion bhajia, vindaloo, katcha korma, roghan josh (with the recommendation to substitute beef if you didn't like lamb). She learned to cook green beans with turmeric, mustard seed, crushed red chilies and the fascinating spice mixture called garam masala, adding a cautionary note that it would be "a touch hot."

She went to see a friend, a teacher in the local high school who had grown up in India, and he shared with her many of his favourite family recipes.

Although he wasn't convinced that authentic Indian dishes could be cooked with less oil than his mother had used because it might interfere with the flavour, Jean persevered, and eventually succeeded in lightening some of her own favourite Indian dishes by reducing the fat content. She also developed a lighter version of the fried milk balls known as gulab jaman.

Wherever they travelled, Jean and Larry seemed to meet people from home, and they collected new friends among ex-patriot Canadians as well as locals. Jean began to see the world as much smaller than she could have imagined on that long-ago day when she took her map to school.

In Bangkok, having dinner with people from Montevideo, Uruguay, she was impressed with one man's assessment of politics in the Americas: "When the United States sneezes, we shake for three weeks."

Coming from Canada, she felt that she understood exactly what he meant.

Although Larry would eventually tire of all the travelling, he spent many years as an enthusiastic companion on her journeys.

"We'd be on the plane heading somewhere, and he'd say, "Well, where'll we go next? After this, where?""

Jean and Larry in formal garb are sitting at a table on the Orient Express, the world's most luxurious train. At Larry's elbow, water is beading on a silver Champagne bucket. It's a taste of Lifestyles of the Rich and Famous, *all the way to Venice.*

For her 70th birthday, Larry bought her the best trip in the world: London to Venice, on the refurbished Orient Express.

After four nights at Claridge's, one of London's finest and fanciest hotels where Jean could scarcely believe the room rates, they took the Orient Express to Venice. It was the ultimate in luxurious travel, with a famous chef on board, serving gourmet cuisine. The exquisite food and white-glove service enchanted Jean, and both she and Larry loved the party atmosphere and found their fellow passengers fascinating.

"The first dinner lasted all the way from London to Folkestone," she recalls. "The turbot was delicious."

In Paris they stayed at the fiercely expensive but exquisitely romantic Hotel Meurice, on the Rue de Rivoli, overlooking the Tuileries Gardens. At the time, executive chef Marc Marchand's steamed filet of John Dory with cinnamon, his potato tart with cèpe mushrooms and his cream of cauliflower soup with smoked eel clams had Parisian gourmets lining up for reservations.

"Eel clams," she says, with a slight shiver. "What is that? I don't think I like the name. Not for me the eel clams, thank you."

In Venice, they were booked into the super-luxe Hotel Cipriani, an Italian palace on its own island, with the sound of water lapping under their window.

Although the cuisine at the Cipriani is classic and the chefs are renowned, most of the time Jean and Larry preferred to prowl the ancient city, wandering through the squares, eating in simple trattorias or pizzerias with menus posted in the windows.

On their last night in Venice it began to rain, so instead of taking the boat across to St. Mark's Square and getting joyfully lost, strolling from bridge to square to fountain as they'd been doing, they decided to stay at the hotel for dinner. There was an Italian dessert she'd been dying to try, just to see if the real thing was better than the Jean Paré version.

In the elegant confines of the Cipriani Bar, her tiny perfect serving of tiramisù cost 28,000 Italian lire.

"In Canadian funds at that time, it was about $28, and I must admit, it was as good as mine," she says. "But not one bit better."

All the travelling had a huge effect on what Jean cooked and how she cooked it, and indeed, how she viewed the entire world of food.

In the wet markets of Bangkok and Hong Kong, among the food shops and at restaurant tables all over Asia, a world of strange new ingredients had opened before her.

Japanese food has always fascinated her for its artistic presentation. In Honolulu, window displays of plastic sushi were like galleries devoted to high realism in food art, and she was amazed at how real it all appeared to be. Although she still cannot force herself to eat any form of raw fish, she appreciates the concept of sushi for its pristine freshness and the perfection of its presentation.

Her husband Larry was a conservative eater, the original meat-and-potatoes guy, and exotic food held few charms for him. Anything highly spiced gave him indigestion.

Jean, on the other hand, would happily try most things. "As long as it wasn't alive and it hadn't suffered." (She balked at live wichiti grubs in Australia and snake in Hong Kong.)

It took Larry years of travelling to accept that his favourite tipple, rye and ginger ale, was not always easy to come by beyond the Canadian border. In England, he found that his simple request often horrified his hosts, who served the British equivalent, scotch, and would go no further than puddling in a little water or a spritz of soda.

Jean's North American travels took her to Disneyland, where she took the greatest delight in eating the giant long-stemmed, chocolate-dipped strawberries, and where her family spotted a display of her cookbooks in a window, "Right beside the Pirates of the Caribbean!

"They were so excited! Amanda told everybody in the crowd that those were her grandma's cookbooks, and they applauded."

Later, while Amanda was a student, perfecting her French at Neuchâtel Junior College in Switzerland, Jean visited her, and was once again thrilled to be part of a home-cooking experience when Amanda's host family made cheese fondue for their guests.

"Fondue was always popular at certain restaurants in the Rockies, but this was in a real Swiss kitchen, and she had a great time," Amanda recalls. "When it appeared in her *Cheese* book, it was the real thing, Swiss family style, with Gruyère cheese, wine, garlic and on the side, the pickles, bread and onions."

When Jean went to New Orleans, she wanted three specific dishes, straight out of an old 1950s rock-a-billy song by Hank Williams: jambalaya, crawfish pie, filé gumbo. For the jambalaya, her best experience was a department store in the French Quarter, where a chef was demonstrating it.

Once again she arrived home with numerous recipes and her own observations and notes, and proceeded to make a version of jambalaya that played well in Vermilion and wherever else her next book, *Dinners of the World*, was sold.

Along with gumbo, sweet potato praline, a Creole salad and a bread pudding with bourbon sauce, she included the rum cocktail known for good reason as a hurricane.

"All that rum livened up the party," she says, but her instinctive caution with alcohol remains.

"When I was testing the hurricane, we poured most of them down the drain."

It was all the travelling that eventually led Jean to another passion: her extended family of foster children.

The numbers change with circumstances, but today Jean supports four children, and has had a total of six; the company has five, and her granddaughter Amanda has always supported one. Jean has met some of her foster children, and corresponds with all of them.

At Christmas, birthdays and throughout the year, she sends letters and cards to Jeselle and Maria-Lyn in the Philippines; Maria-Lovellie, Rachelle and a boy named Peggy in Haiti; Ahmed in Egypt; Shakila in Tanzania; Jiao in China; and Omar-Oklides in El Salvador.

During the filming of a documentary on her life, Jean visited her Haitian children. She was travelling with Amanda, and the two women were shocked by the poverty, but impressed with the quiet dignity of the people.

"In the villages, they simply have no infrastructure. No road maintenance, no garbage disposal, limited resources in every way. Their lives seem very hard."

While she was there, the families of her foster children celebrated with a festive dinner of chicken, beans and rice. They cooked while she and Amanda watched, but they decided not to eat the food, even though it was offered.

"They needed it themselves. It was an extravagance for them, using a whole chicken. I know it was more than they could afford, and I thought, how generous of them," she says. "How very generous."

Some people have cautioned her about this kind of charity, and she always listens politely.

"I've been told by a few skeptics that the money doesn't go to the people who need it most, and that there are rip-offs within the system.

"But I've visited these people, and I've seen the good that even a small amount can do. I say, if one or two people are ripping me off, that's on their conscience, not mine. All I care about is the children."

September 2004. At the Cuisine Canada convention, subtitled Northern Bounty, Jean is called to the platform in a Kelowna ballroom to accept a special award for her lifelong contribution to food in Canada.

But there have been recent hurricanes in Haiti, and her thoughts tonight are with three children in a ruined village: Maria-Lovellie, Rachelle and a boy named Peggy.

Her opening remarks are for them.

"While we're all enjoying this northern bounty, Haiti is suffering," she says, with her heart in her words, her voice ringing with emotion.

"Please help. Our hope lies with our children."

SIX

JUST DESSERT
How sweet it is

Shortly after the beginning of her eighteen-year catering career, Jean began keeping meticulous records of what she cooked, what worked, what didn't and what changes she'd make the next time around.

Her habit was to write her menu on a single scribbler page, in longhand, and after the event, she'd record all the leftovers on the next page, along with her comments. Gradually, she accumulated many volumes of catering wisdom, and filed it all away in several cardboard boxes.

Although neither she nor her clients were truly aware of it, Jean had one special quality that set her apart from the average catering company: she loved a party, whether it was hers or someone else's. Her natural sociability was a huge plus, and she continued to build her catering business by over-delivering on every event. She was especially lavish with bridal parties.

"I always gave the wedding parties more than they expected," she says. "Brides have enough to worry about, without something going wrong on the catering end. I wanted it to be perfect for them."

Jean's recipe sources were always wide-ranging, collected over many years from her long association with the traditional cooks in her own family, or from other good cooks who simply wanted to share.

Still others were the found objects from her travels, like the New Zealand casserole with sausage meat, oddly named the Viennese puff.

"I got the recipe during a visit to Auckland, and the woman who gave it to me has become a friend. We still write to each other, all these years later."

During the catering years, it was a rare event if, after the meal had been served, there weren't at least two or three guests appearing at the kitchen door to buttonhole Jean and ask for a recipe, or maybe two. They were usually women, and they found her to be entirely approachable.

"One night at a wedding dance, the girls in the kitchen were betting on the number of these requests," Grant recalls. "And soon there were twelve people at the door, asking for recipes."

Unlike those grand professional chefs who either flatly refuse to part with a recipe or merrily hand out badly amended versions of the real thing, Jean not only shared her recipes, but was thrilled to sit down right there and then and write them out by hand.

"There wasn't always time to do that, so I was happy to mail out a few recipes. It was a two-way street, because they'd often share their own recipes with me."

She had no sense of secrecy or personal ownership. Good food was all about sharing, and she was happy to do it. She was also scrupulously honest about ingredients and methods.

"I'd never pass on a recipe I wouldn't use myself," she says.

It was probably inevitable that she would decide to put them all together in a book. It just made sense.

"People kept telling me I should write a cookbook, and I did have five big cardboard boxes full of recipe clippings, but I never seemed to get around to the book itself. It was a very slow procedure, I found."

Jean was one of those rare, lucky people who discover their particular passion early in life. For some, the passion is writing, painting, or coaxing orchids to bloom in an inhospitable northern climate. But for Jean, cooking was her passion. Even when other aspects of her life seemed to be in chaos, she found the culinary arts to be totally absorbing and compelling.

She read cookbooks like novels, mentally tasting, then trying the best ones in her own kitchen. She had a particular fondness for community cookbooks, church cookbooks, Junior League cookbooks, anything written by those homemaking women she considered to be the real cooks in North America, and indeed everywhere else she travelled in the world.

"There's often a name there, of the person who submitted the recipe. They likely have to cook the same way I do. It makes them seem like everyday people to me."

As it is with many cookbooks that are essentially collections of favourite dishes, Jean's first book would be a slice of personal history, inspired by remembered flavours and aromas forever tied to time and place. They reflected her own prairie background, and that of the traditional bakers and cooks in her family.

For Jean, the urge to write her first cookbook was founded on her love of simple cooking, and the pleasure it had always given her. The smell of roast beef on Sunday and the sweet-spicy aroma of simmering chow-chow during canning season had always meant good times, in a kitchen where she was surrounded by love. That strong sense of family was part of her memory bank, and was always associated with food.

In her first book, it would be the near-incense of cinnamon/nutmeg/cloves in a pan of raisin spice bars, or the visual pleasure of a three-tiered silver cake tray, holding twenty-seven different varieties of her own home-baked creations, that inspired her. These were the special treats offered up at formal teas or wedding receptions in small-town Canada. They evoked happy times and gentle celebrations where friends and neighbours drank their coffee from bone china cups and used their Sunday manners.

Another time, another place, and Jean's raw materials and motivation might have been entirely different, but this was no Paris-trained Julia Child, in pursuit of the perfect foie gras or oysters Rockefeller.

The Julia Child tomes were too big and expensive, and frankly, a multi-page recipe for croissants wasn't of much interest to Jean, who'd much rather bake, and write about, overnight refrigerator rolls or air buns. Still, they had some things in common.

"I remember seeing Julia Child on *Larry King Live*, talking about how cilantro was suddenly so over-used. I think she said if she found a piece of it on her plate, she'd throw it on the floor.

"That's exactly how I feel about cilantro. If you add salt to a dish, it enhances the flavour of whatever you're cooking, whether it's carrots or beef. But if you add cilantro, that's what you taste — cilantro."

Neither was Jean an earlier version of a Martha Stewart, spinning every available domestic skill from bed-making to gardening into yet another business deal, although she was probably capable of doing so, and had learned to survive a disastrous marriage by using her own innate financial savvy in a number of profitable real estate deals.

Did she want security? Was it the old Mark Twain admonition, "Buy land, they're not making it anymore"? Whatever the reason, in the next two decades, she would buy and sell a number of properties.

For Jean, who had no formal training as a commercial chef and had spent no significant time in any cooking school beyond her mother's kitchen, the theory and practice of the larger food world was still unfolding.

In 1980, at fifty-three years of age, she'd never tasted capers, never cooked an artichoke, or eaten truffles, nor had she done any extensive tastings of trendy ingredients like olive oils or flavoured vinegars. Her father had loved blue cheese, and managed to bring some home now and then, as an adult treat. Jean, however, hadn't tasted any variety of blue cheese until she got to England, where she was introduced to her very first Stilton. It was a love match from the first bite, but it didn't always work that way for her.

Sometimes eating, let alone cooking the foods that have become part of culinary pop culture, has been a challenge.

"I never ate a shrimp until I was forty, and even then it was tough to do," she says. "They looked like cutworms to me."

So did fiddleheads. Oysters were pretty well unthinkable, especially raw ones, though her father and her Prince Edward Island-raised mother had been crazy about oysters, and somehow arranged to have them as a special treat every Christmas.

Jean didn't think they were a treat, and flatly refused to eat them.

"They're slimy," she declared, and no matter how many glittering restaurants she's been in since, or how many chefs have tried to tempt her, she can't bring herself to eat a raw oyster.

"Not mussels, either," she says. "They look just like chicken lungs."

Because many of the chefs she meets wouldn't actually recognize a chicken's lung if they tripped over it, they cannot disagree.

She also detested innards of any kind. No tongue, liver, brains, sweetbreads, heart or kidney would she eat, and she wasn't inclined to cook them either.

"I'd seen animals butchered," she says. "I didn't want anything from their insides unless it came in a shell. Eggs were a different matter."

When Gail brought an escargot shell home from a dinner party so her mother could get a whiff of the delicious garlic butter and see how good it might taste, Jean defeated her argument with simple country-style logic.

"You could cook a mouse in that sauce, and it would probably taste just fine," she reasoned.

But, with her prairie sensibility of waste not, want not and a background rich in homecooking, she knew good food when she tasted it. Although she was always curious and would try almost anything once, she had a tendency to dismiss anything too fussy or exotic.

"She doesn't put on the dog," says her son, Grant. "Mom doesn't do flashy."

For awhile, like many aspiring authors, Jean's cookbook project lacked focus. She dithered over what to write, which recipes to include. There were already so many cookbooks, what did she have to offer that would be different enough to attract the kind of audience she wanted? It was Grant, a marketing graduate with a job in an oil company, who helped her decide on a course of action.

"Concentrate on one book," he said. "One subject."

Always ready to listen to advice from her family, she mulled over the possibilities. Stew, soup, bread, cake ...

"It needed to be something everybody loved. The most popular item, the one for which I got the most requests, was any kind of square, or bar, which was really the same thing but cut in rectangles. They were especially popular at showers and church teas, and they were real money-makers at bake sales."

They were also the recipes she was always handing out by request.

After every wedding supper there was a dance, and late in the evening, after the musicians had packed up or at least slowed down for a break, she'd roll out the midnight lunch: sandwiches, coffee and tray after tray of squares, ten different varieties cut into small pieces and beautifully arranged with a certain mathematical precision. The guests found them irresistible: cherry squares, double brownies, Nanaimo bars, chocolate cherry creams, butterscotch confetti roll, fruit roll, tropical treat, snow log, raisin quickie, fudgy macaroons, apricot roll ...

The squares were always a huge hit. Some guests would sample one of each, then ask Jean for a couple of recipes.

Squares it would be, then. Never one to settle for halfway measures in any project, Jean cut back on her catering, keeping only the odd wedding and the Vermilion high school graduations, which were a labour of love.

In 1980, she turned Gail's old bedroom into an office and went to work on her first cookbook, testing the recipes for *150 Delicious Squares* — her working title.

"Nanaimo bars were originally called smog bars, and everybody made them: graham-cracker crust, cocoa, Bird's Eye custard in the filling. My Grandma Locke made smog bars, so did my mother. Brownies are also generations old, though I felt like a traitor because I used cocoa in mine instead of melted chocolate, like Mom's. Nut smacks were from Grandma Locke, and matrimonial squares, also called date squares, were just a good old recipe with no particular pedigree."

Everybody had a few recipes for squares tucked away somewhere, but Jean's extensive collection was unique for its size and scope.

For her first book, she tested 177 different squares, hoping to end up with 150 keepers. Some were too similar to warrant the extra space. Others were too complicated, or too exotic, or too expensive to make. In the keepers, melting chocolate was replaced by cocoa whenever possible, being cheaper and, she reasoned, available in any kitchen cupboard. Anything with hard-to-find ingredients got the boot, so while crushed pineapple was in, macadamia nuts were out.

By this time Grant and Frieda were living in Saskatoon. One day, driving to Saskatoon for a book-planning visit, Jean had been making lists of possible cookbook names. She was thinking about her mother, Ruby Elford, and how she would yell up the stairs, "Company's coming," and how exciting that was.

That's when she knew she had The Name.

"I rang Grant's doorbell, and as soon as he answered, I blurted out, "Company's Coming!"

"I know," he said. "And here you are."

"No, I mean the book. Let's call it Company's Coming!"

Having invested in several revenue properties, Jean now sold one of her houses to finance the first book. She figured $50,000 would cover the ingredients for all the squares, the cost of photography and the printing, and keep her car on the road, running back and forth between Vermilion and Saskatoon. Grant was in from the first; she had seventy-five per cent, he had twenty-five per cent of their new business venture.

While preparing to launch yet another career, this time as a self-publisher, Jean got busy and made a list of everything she didn't like about cookbooks in general.

They were cumbersome. They wouldn't stay open. They used too many ingredients she didn't usually have on hand, and there simply weren't enough pictures, so she was often disappointed when what came out of the oven didn't look like she'd expected.

She also knew what she wanted in a working cookbook, and was willing to bet that her potentially huge audience of home cooks would agree with her.

A good cookbook needed a generous, easy-to-read typeface, with imperial measure first, and because it was a Canadian book, it would be followed by metric measurements on the same line.

It had to have a plastic comb binding, so the title would be readable on a bookshelf but the book would lie flat on the kitchen counter, and page numbers had to be on the outside corner.

"I don't care whether it's at the bottom of the page or the top, but I will not have it stuck in an inside corner. Do you know how hard it is to find a specific page when the number is hidden like that?"

The recipes had to be scaled to the home kitchen, and that included the equipment and appliances she used for testing the recipes. There were very few professional six-burner Garland gas ranges in home kitchens across Canada, so she deliberately kept her *batterie de cuisine* pared to the bone, though she did have an extra second-hand electric stove and an industrial-sized fridge in the garage, the legacy of her successful catering career.

In her first book, Jean insisted on a colour photograph for every recipe. Everything should look ready to serve, with no cosmetic trickery involved, no shaving foam whipped cream or lacquered cherries.

She also insisted on a food map, a clearly labelled diagram to identify each item on each plate by number.

More importantly in those first books, every recipe had to be made with ordinary ingredients that would, in her opinion, be found in the average kitchen or, failing that, one quick trip to the nearest supermarket.

As with her catering career, in becoming a publisher Jean was to some extent shooting in the dark. She didn't actually know the difference between a printer and a publisher.

When she discovered that publishers would bear all the expense but would also own the rights to her book, and would pay her only a standard royalty, she knew she'd have to self-publish, because it was the only way she could maintain control of her book.

She had no idea about the logistics of the publishing business, or even that 5,000 books was considered a bestseller in this country. She signed her initial contract with Centax, a printer/publisher in Regina that specialized in package deals on cookbooks, and blithely ordered an unprecedented 15,000 copies.

"In our first book, we leaned toward the traditional cooking of our home — my mother, my grandmothers. That's still our core. But we've expanded well beyond traditional food. People travel constantly, they're all over the world, and what we can buy here has also changed. These days everybody sells couscous and capers."

Later, following the launch of Company's Coming *Casseroles*, a reader would complain that several of Jean's recipes involved tins of cream-of-mushroom soup, which wasn't real cooking. Jean didn't argue, but she offered a suggestion.

"If you don't want to use canned soup, you could always make the mushroom soup from scratch," she said. "You know — start with fresh mushrooms, a little onion, butter, flour, cream, salt, pepper ..."

"I'd never have time," sniffed the busy reader.

"Exactly," Jean replied.

When it was finally time to take the photographs for *Squares,* Jean spent two weeks baking and freezing yet another round of her 170-plus top choices, including Grant's personal favourite, Seafoam Chews—later renamed Grant's Special—and Frieda's Number 89, a chewy, spicy cranberry bar. She loaded them all in the cavernous trunk of the Mercury, and headed for Saskatoon with her arsenal of white banquet paper, flexible spatulas, knives and all the paraphernalia for icing dozens and dozens of squares. She also carted in most of the props, from silver cake servers to three-tiered trays.

"We covered the basement floor of Grant and Frieda's home with white banquet paper, iced and garnished all the squares, and cut them. It took hours and hours, and it was back-breaking work, bending over for so long. Then we drove them to the studio, where we styled the shots. We arranged them on serving plates, and the photographer went to work."

It took two full days. When it was over, they called all the neighbours and divvied up the goodies.

One neighbour, who didn't know you could freeze squares, ate most of them right away.

"Can you imagine ordering 15,000 books for that initial run of *Squares*? I didn't know any better. Ignorance was bliss back then."

She was fifty-three years old, and about to launch her fresh new career in one of the world's most competitive and cutthroat businesses: book publishing.

Her next hurdle was the most important thing any author has to do: sell the book. She started with a local druggist, a man named Brent Long whom she'd known since he was a kid in high school. He ordered a whole case. It was her first sale, and she's never forgotten it.

But they weren't all as friendly or as sensitive as Brent Long. At her next call, in another town, the manager of one store rifled through the book and laughed at her. She felt like crying, but she went back to her car more determined than ever.

During the next six months, Jean hit the road with a trunk full of books and a highly original marketing plan devised by Grant. She would sell *150 Delicious*

Squares where no cookbooks had gone before: in gas stations, drugstores, grocery stores, hair salons, department stores.

"I knew I had to get them out there. It doesn't matter how good your book is ... if the public doesn't see it, you won't sell it."

When Jean attended her first book fair in Vancouver, she had Gail with her. They were both delighted to discover Gail's natural ability to sell. Jean had another edge: she was handing out samples of the squares from her cookbook. For the time and place, it was a first.

"People found a reason to stop by," she says modestly. She knew the power of a good square.

Before the 1981 book fair ended, she and Gail had opened 57 accounts.

That meant more months and miles of travel. Jean covered the prairies in her own car, serving a growing list of regular accounts while beating the bushes for new customers. But it paid off.

The first edition of 15,000 copies, printed April 1981, sold out in three months.

The second edition, September 1981, was 25,000 copies, a huge print run by Canadian standards.

For the third edition, October 1981, they bumped the run up to 50,000.

The fourth edition, in June 1982, was another 50,000 copies.

150 Delicious Squares would go on to sell over one million copies.

Jean, with Grant and Gail beside her, is surrounded by displays of her books. The family is smiling hopefully. "Have a brownie? Try it. You'll like it!"

A year later they attended the Canadian Booksellers Show in Toronto, and this time Grant went along. They had two titles on their table, Jean's book on *Squares* plus her second book, *Casseroles.*

The mainstream publishing industry in North America is like a ruthless lover, seducing authors one month, discarding them the next, sometimes leaving them dangling for months.

Grant remembers their first encounter with a major eastern publisher.

"He was a heavy-set guy representing a New York firm. He approached our table, ate a square, picked up a copy of the book, and said, 'What are you doing with this?'

"We told him. She writes; we publish and distribute.

"He looked around, set the book down, and said, 'Let me explain something to you. There are publishers and there are distributors. You can't be both.'

"Then, punctuating each word by punching his index finger onto the book, he said, 'You have to decide which one you want to be.'"

By this time, Jean and Grant were both feeling a touch downcast, even embarrassed, but their advisor wasn't finished.

"He picked up *Squares* again and said, 'Okay, let me tell you what I mean. How many of these have you sold?'

"Mom and I looked at each other and gulped, and I said, 'Uh, well, just over 200,000 copies so far.'"

Neither Jean nor Grant knew whether he'd approve or not, so they waited, wondering just how bad their sales figures might look to a big New York publishing executive.

"He stood motionless for a long second," Grant recalls. "Then he let the book fall back on the table. He wheeled around, and walked away without saying another word.

"We took it that we hadn't done so badly after all."

Still, the Toronto incident was typical of an attitude that prevailed among mainstream publishers. The big ones who noticed Jean at all saw a pleasant, friendly woman with a self-published, coil-bound cookbook being promoted and sold by her family. They were cordial to her face, but privately, they shook their heads.

No cutting-edge trends, no flashy new food fad to hang a publicity campaign on, and to make matters funnier, she was from someplace called Vermilion, Alberta. Most of them had never heard of it.

Naive-woman-with-kids-and-cookbook. It was almost laughable.

Somewhere around the time when Jean sold her one-millionth cookbook, they would all stop laughing.

During those first years, when she wasn't on the road, Jean managed shipping and receiving and fired off orders and invoices. All the while, her food-loving nature was urging her on. With Grant increasingly taking the lead, she soon realized that what she wanted was not one book, not two, but a series. A long-running, comprehensive series of easy-to-use, affordably collectible cookbooks. About 160 pages in a six by nine-inch format. With lots of colour photography. All under the Company's Coming imprint.

Jean became a one-woman recipe factory, collecting, testing, writing and rewriting recipes, at her own expense in her own kitchen.

As *150 Delicious Squares* continued to sell, Jean moved on to her next cookbook. They produced *Casseroles*, a collection of recipes for one-dish comfort food. Then she jumped on the muffin trend with *Muffins & More*, incorporating a number of recipes for quick breads.

Grant remembers those days.

"At first, Mom was Company's Coming. But as the business grew, she became more focused on the recipes, and I took over the business end."

Jean, too, recalls.

"Grant tried to help me, working weekends and holidays, but he was in Saskatoon and I was in Vermilion.

"Within eighteen months, I'd hired five people for packing, shipping and general office work, and I still wasn't getting the time I needed to research, write and test my recipes for the books.

"Finally, he decided to take over the business part of it, leaving me free to do what I did best — work with the recipes. My son left a promising career to join me full-time. Without that decision, Company's Coming would have been a whole lot smaller than it is."

▲ Larry and Jean
dine in style on the
Orient Express, 1998.

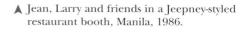

▲ Jean, Larry and friends in a Jeepney-styled
restaurant booth, Manila, 1986.

▲ Jean makes a personal delivery
to a Singapore chef, 1996.

Jean with Bob Hope ➤
and Alice Soldan at
Brian's Reno swap
meet, 1983.

▲ Jean visits one of
her Haitian foster
children, 2002.

◄ Visiting the family
of another foster
child, Haiti, 2002.

Jean in Haiti with ➤
foster son Peggy,
Peggy's mother and
Jean's granddaughter
Amanda, 2002.

▲ The chocolate obsession is with her still: Jean, on location for a TV shoot in Atlantic Canada during a *Chocolate Everything* publicity tour, 2000.

▲ *Dinners of the World* — Helen Urwin, Jean and Grant, 1990.

◄ Kathy Knowles and Jean at *Casseroles* photo shoot, 1981.

◄ Stephe Tate, photographer, with Jean at *Microwave Cooking* shoot, 1992.

▲ Jean gets a little help from the Cookie Monster at the launch of *Cookies*, 1988.

▲ Staff celebrating ten million books sold, Edmonton, 1995.

(Clockwise from left) Grant,▶ Jean, Brian, Lyall, Gail, celebrating the first million books sold, 1985.

▲ Jean and Grant at a book signing in Halifax, 1984.

◀ Larry and Jean at the family dinner celebrating the first million books sold.

Photo: Richard Siemens

▲ Office portrait, 1993 (clockwise from left): Brian, Lyall, Gail, Grant.

Photo: Stephe Tate Photo

▲ A surprise for Jean. Grown-up version of a childhood portrait: Gail, Grant, Brian, Lyall.

91

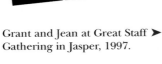

◄ Jean gets another saxophone, presented by family at a party for the ten-millionth book sold, 1995.

Grant and Jean at Great Staff ➤ Gathering in Jasper, 1997.

▲ Grant, Jean and Gail in San Antonio, Texas. Sales meeting, 1996.

Camera taking aim at Jean ➤ and Janice Ryan on set of *Company's Coming Everyday Cooking* television show, 1996.

Welcome to Irma sign located on ➤
Highway 14 east of town, erected in
Jean's honour for her school reunion.

◀ Ryan Hildebrand,
Grant, Jean and David
Friesen during a party
in Altona, Manitoba,
celebrating 20 years of
Friesens printing
Company's Coming
cookbooks.

▼ Jean and Larry at the Harvest Gala,
Calgary, 2004.

▲ Jean with a few fans
during a Saskatoon
trade show.

▲ (Left to right) Gail, Amanda, Jean, wearing the insignia of Member of the Order of Canada, and Frieda following presentation ceremonies at Rideau Hall in Ottawa, 2005.

Jean hosts a family tea ➤ at the Empress Hotel in Victoria, 2004.

▲ Jean with the coffee group in her Vermilion kitchen.

SEVEN

ICING ON THE CAKE

 I f the big eastern food publishers ignored Jean — and they did, at first — the hometown crowd adored her from the beginning. Soon they'd be joined by enthusiastic Jean Paré fans all over the world.

Company's Coming earned that loyal following as they capitalized on a growing trend for single-subject cookbooks. Collectors loved Jean.

In 1983, for her third book, Grant added a second printer. It's probably no coincidence that he signed on with the very successful family printing operation, Friesens, in Altona, Manitoba.

David Friesen is the senior partner, chairman and chief executive officer in their 100-year-old family business. At the time, his company was geared to working with mid-sized to large publishers, and manufacturing the finished product after it had been fully designed. Dealing with Jean and her family was a unique experience for them.

As a printer, he's only too familiar with the term "vanity press," the name mainstream publishers and those in the book business give to self-publishers like Jean and Grant.

"Yes, I hear it every day. Traditional publishers still look askance at that. Yet some of our best, most successful customers are people who originate and publish their own work."

Jean and company were doing just that, in spades. *Salads* came next, hot, cold or frozen, followed by *Appetizers,* hot, cold, plain or fancy.

"Grant and Frieda talked me into putting snails in the *Appetizers* book," she says. "I still didn't like the way they looked, but I agreed to use their recipe if they taste-tested it."

Jean, shopping for pasta in Edmonton's Italian Centre Shop, is buying every brand and every shape in the store. Owner Frank Spinelli, watching from his office above the shop, can hardly believe his eyes. He rushes down to help this unusual customer lug over 100 packages of pasta to her car. She tells him she's testing a few recipes.

Next she launched *Soups & Sandwiches*, followed by *Cookies*, then *Pasta*, then *Barbecues*. It seemed she couldn't put a foot wrong. No matter what the topic, her fans kept snapping them up.

With the publication of *Preserves*, she recognized a contemporary trend for small-quantity canning, now that families and gardens were no longer as large as they'd once been.

She wrote *Kids Cooking*, a title many of her fans had been waiting for. *Cooking for Two* followed, then came *Breakfasts & Brunches*, and a timely collection called *Slow Cooker Recipes*. (They've since done a second collection for the handy counter-top appliance called the slow cooker.)

Jean was on a roll with Grant as president and her daughter, Gail, as vice president in charge of marketing and distribution. Eventually Grant's daughter, Amanda, would handle communications and media bookings for Jean's burgeoning career. Company's Coming was making established publishers — especially those who once wouldn't have given her a second glance — scratch their heads and wonder. What was her secret?

David Friesen gives full credit to Grant Lovig for understanding the key to book marketing.

"You didn't just plop the book on a bookshelf. You had to place it where the people go. Grant designed these very effective display racks that were unique at the time, and have since been copied by other publishers."

Today Jean's books are distributed through regional and national chains, as well as independent retailers, where they're prominently displayed in the Grant-designed purpose-built racks. In stores that have traditionally sold everything from mallets to makeup, but not, specifically, cookbooks, Company's Coming became a given. The books endeared themselves to retailers, and were often placed in the best of all possible spots — close to the cash register — in more than 6,000 retail outlets, from the Bay and Chapters to Wal-Mart and Zellers, and everything that comes between.

Initially, their relationship with Friesens was strictly about production, but then Jean decided to go to Altona, visit the plant and meet the staff. There was coffee. There were trays of squares. She remembers it well.

"They really rolled out the red carpet for us," she says. "They couldn't have been nicer, or made us feel more welcome."

That day, she autographed books and visited with everyone from the plant. It was a typical Jean touch, one she carried into major celebrations for every milestone. That included the huge parties they dubbed Great Staff Gatherings, held anywhere from Jasper National Park to her own home in Vermilion.

"From the beginning, we've always been fortunate with our staff," she says. "They've been more like family. I never wanted to feel that I was working with strangers. You know how it is — you just want to get to know people."

Friesen saw that side of Jean and her children.

"When we'd travel to Edmonton, we'd often have meals with Grant and Frieda, and Jean was always included," says Friesen. "We'd been in business for nearly 100 years, and had done many cookbooks of different kinds, including one for my mother and her group, which ultimately became the bestselling *Canadian Mennonite Cookbook.*

"But nothing was like Company's Coming. They were always multiples. One book a year became two, and then there were the reprints. Jean and Grant were their own cookbook production company. They've been a big part of our growth, and among our largest customers for the last twenty years."

One year, Friesen's had a picnic at the Altona Centennial Park, with 500 employees plus all their families. The mayor arrived to present Jean with the key to the city and declare her an honourary citizen of Altona. It was a proud moment for her.

In the Edmonton headquarters of Company's Coming, a blue appliquéd quilt hangs in the main stairwell. The pattern is the exquisitely detailed cover of Jean's first book, *150 Delicious Squares.* It was Friesens' gift to Company's Coming, on the occasion of their 20th anniversary, in 2001.

"Grant and Jean always celebrated special anniversaries and events with the entire company, and in the past, we had given them small gifts to mark the occasion," says David Friesen. "But for their 20th anniversary, we had this quilt especially designed. Jean surrounds herself with family, and they all get along. She's one-of-a-kind. We thought the quilt was a fitting memento."

By this time, Jean had done several thousand media interviews, received numerous awards and honours, and was definitely the star of what had evolved into a kind of Company's Coming road show, criss-crossing the country to speak here and be presented there. She was a model spokesperson, always happy to climb on another plane and meet another group of fans. Oddly, beneath the genuine warmth of Jean's public face, there was still a reserved and rather shy woman, wondering what all the fuss was about.

By August of 1995, Company's Coming had published 25 single-subject titles and 5 mini-books, with more than $100 million in retail sales from 10 million cookbooks. They were churning out three or more new titles per year, all of them handwritten by Jean in the first draft.

Their numbers were staggering: 7,000 accounts, and not just in Canada. Jean's books were also selling in the U.S., Australia, New Zealand, Singapore, Japan and Europe, and they'd been translated into French and, for the Mexican market, Spanish.

As 2001 came to a close, Jean and company had published 60 titles and sold 17 million copies.

Still, from the mid '80s into the next decade, they were almost running to catch up with their own success. In 1985, when Jean's test kitchen needs outgrew her own home, she built a two-bedroom bungalow in Vermilion specifically for that use. Using lessons of the past, she planned for the future: "I thought when I didn't need it as a test kitchen anymore, I could sell it as a family home."

Meanwhile, the company's administration and distribution operations relocated to Edmonton for better access to facilities, staff and transportation links. Grant, by now living in Edmonton, was back and forth every time a new title was ready to be captured on film. It was a punishing schedule, but they were having fun.

"We were still doing all the photography for the books ourselves, and a photo shoot would typically last three days, eight a.m. to midnight, plus the time it took to set up and tear down," he recalls.

"Mom would be upstairs prepping food for the shots with help from two of her friends, Linda Donily and Helen Urwin, who was also Company's Coming's first employee. I'd supervise the shoot downstairs, in the basement studio.

"Each shoot meant gathering a lot of the food and props in Edmonton, hauling it all out to Vermilion, unloading the whole thing and running it down to the basement studio. Then we'd set up, select the props, style the food, shoot the pictures, tear down and reload the truck for the drive back to Edmonton."

Grant was doing the work of half a dozen technical specialists, but he had a good eye for colour and form, and somehow he pulled it off. But it was time and labour intensive, and by 1994, the sheer volume of photography and recipe testing had outgrown the small bungalow in Vermilion.

So the following year, in 1995, Company's Coming opened a state-of-the-art test kitchen and photo studio called The Recipe Factory, a five-minute drive from their home office in south Edmonton. They started with 2,700 square feet, and in 2001 took over the adjoining bay, doubling their space and gaining a lot more elbow room. It included a large, bright, well-equipped test kitchen, an editorial suite, a prop room and a photo studio.

It was no longer just Jean and Grant. As the physical size of the production grew, the staff grew apace.

"Today, we produce many more titles, eight to ten a year," says Grant. "We look for marketing opportunities, such as the growing need for cookbooks among people with diabetes. Then we design a product to meet those needs. We maintain an idea pool, categorize them, keeping in mind that fads don't last, but trends are important."

Like father, like daughter, like son: over a period of twenty years, Jean and Grant spun Company's Coming cookbooks into a series of business ventures. They were all designed to promote her books and the Company's Coming name, and would eventually include several different foodservice operations, a television show and a food magazine.

One example of the foodservice operations was a series of kiosks selling baked goods. Franchising was the new wave. From cookies to muffins to cinnamon buns, specialty bakeries were hot.

Considering the popularity of Jean's books, especially her *Squares* book, the family reasoned that if they were to offer a variety of homestyle baking — loaves, cookies, her ever-popular squares — in a mall setting, shoppers and office workers, especially those in the downtown core, would line up to buy. People who didn't have the time or even the skills to bake at home would be their potential market.

It seemed like a natural fit.

The first kiosk opened in Calgary and response was good. Soon they had a chain of 25 franchised outlets, selling baked goods in malls across Canada.

January 2005. Over the ever-present cup of coffee in the boardroom of the

Company's Coming home office, Grant talks about what happened, with the easy fluency of one who has said it all before.

Jean is also at the table, and every now and then she interjects with a comment or an opinion.

They both remember an unexpected hitch in the plan.

"Mom's recipes didn't necessarily work well commercially," Grant offers.

With the reputation of her recipes somehow in question, Jean interjects. "The recipes — *my* recipes — were not the problem," she says firmly.

"You see, we had hired a professional baker in Calgary, where we had a central commissary. The products were supposed to taste like they'd been made following my recipe, but they didn't, because he hadn't used the ingredients I used, the regular butter, eggs and so forth that we all have in our kitchens."

She pauses, but any halfway competent scriptwriter could have predicted the next move in this little saga.

"He was substituting commercial ingredients, and the result was that they didn't taste homemade," she says, recipes vindicated. "That's the truth."

So they changed the product mix, and began making fewer squares and more small loaf cakes. They added a few lunch items to attract the crowd who ate in the malls where their cafes were located. It was more in line with what they had envisioned in the first place, but eventually Jean and Grant no longer had an interest in the cafes, neither literally nor figuratively.

There would be other enterprises of a similar nature, including a brief involvement with Domino's Pizza, but eventually both Jean and Grant realized that retail foodservice was not the best exposure for Company's Coming books. And that, after all, was what they were about. Had been, from the first 15,000 copies of *Squares*, and planned to be, as long as there was a demand for Jean's books.

Then came food television.

"When we moved into television in the mid '90s, the purpose, once again, was exposure for Mom's books," Grant recalls.

The timing looked good. The American Food Network launched in 1993 and the early lineups had no blockbusters. Emeril and his "Bam!" philosophy wouldn't catch fire until 1997 and the industry was still a long way from producing an Iron Chef. Maybe there was a place for a down-home Canadian cooking show.

Company's Coming Everyday Cooking didn't feature a big-name chef or a celebrity host, and the format was a familiar one in cooking shows of that era.

It opened with a tinkly piano theme as the camera swept through the dining room, hovered briefly over a perfectly set table, travelled on to a well-appointed, plant-filled kitchen, and finally zoomed in on the host, a friendly blonde actress named Janice Ryan.

Janice would do a brief "Welcome to the Company's Coming kitchen" monologue. Another actor, Mario Trono, was her co-star and comic relief, interacting with both Janice and Jean, popping up in both kitchens — the Company's Coming kitchen studio set, and another, completely separate set, for Jean's Kitchen.

Recipes from two or three of Jean's books were demonstrated on each show, and references to the volume and page number were flashed on the screen before each commercial break.

Jean's appearances had been limited to short vignettes with Mario, during which she might show him a gadget such as an egg slicer, and see if he could guess how to use it. Then she'd demonstrate it. Her total time on camera was about 90 seconds.

Not nearly long enough for her fans, it seemed. Famous author though she was, she was also a woman this viewing audience could relate to, and they were far more interested in watching Jean than a host they didn't know.

"After the first season, viewers let us know there was something missing," Grant recalls. "They wanted to see more of Mom."

In the second season it was decided that Jean would do one complete show out of five, with Mario doing his funny-but-inept bit, and Jean coming to his rescue before he could massacre the meal.

"Mom was more than willing to cooperate. She'd done thousands of interviews, and when the cameras rolled, she tried hard."

If anything, she appeared to be trying too hard, and her performance lacked the familiar comfort level of her books.

"I enjoyed it, I really did," Jean insists. "But it was frustrating. It took so much time. Just when Mario and I would finally get it right, a plane would go over, or there'd be some other glitch, and we'd have to do a retake."

Grant recalls her days in front of the camera.

"Mom did enjoy working on the show for the most part. I felt for her though, because she was out of her element. Some people are naturals for TV, but Mom is not a showman."

At this point Jean starts to protest, but he continues.

"Mom, you were never the woman who left home with your basket of muffins, determined to become a TV star."

Then he adds a hasty amendment.

"You're a real trooper, Mom. You'd walk over hot coals for us if we asked, and we all know that. But television just wasn't right for you."

Company's Coming Everyday Cooking ran for two full seasons, then went into reruns.

Next up, a further venture in publishing. Again, it was planned as exposure for the Company's Coming brand, and in April of 2001, a new magazine arrived on Canada's newsstands. Grant Lovig's name was on the masthead as publisher, and Jean was listed as a regular columnist.

Cooking at Home: Canada's Own Recipe Magazine had an initial print run of 100,000. It was a colourful magazine with page after page of glossy food photography. Each issue was stuffed with reader-friendly information and recipes from all across Canada.

And there on page 10 was everybody's favourite, the *Ask Jean* column, where she'd answer questions and dispense kitchen wisdom about wide-ranging culinary problems such as tempering chocolate or keeping pickles crisp.

The magazine had an instant national audience.

Readers loved it, and they said so. For awhile, it seemed that *Cooking at Home* might at last be the dialogue on food that no other Canadian publisher had successfully managed, though several had tried.

Sadly, it didn't last. In a press release announcing the demise of *Cooking at Home*, Grant noted that the problem was not in the results, but in the cost of attaining them.

"Despite the overwhelmingly positive response from our readers, it would have taken another two to five years to break even," he told the assembled staff in the Company's Coming office. "The magazine is sucking money faster than we can make it. Our pockets simply are not deep enough."

"It lasted one year," he says. "Seven issues."

Brief though the magazine venture was, it did succeed on several levels, as did the television show. In the style typical of Jean and her family, they chalked it up to another entrepreneurial experience, and moved on. The core activity of their company was, and would continue to be, cookbooks.

In 2002, Jean was in her mid-seventies and going strong, fully occupied with generating new ideas and helping produce several cookbooks a year.

That was the year her life story went public, when the Idea Factory produced a one-hour documentary, *The Recipe for Success*, as part of their Life and Times series. It aired on CBC, CBC Newsworld and later on the Biography Channel.

"It felt odd," she says. "I couldn't figure out why anybody would be interested."

Jean's company had started with 150 homey recipes, one slim book and 15,000 copies, sold through small independent retailers. In twenty-five years, there would be 13,000 recipes, over 100 books and 23 million copies, sold nationally and internationally.

Company's Coming had become a publishing phenomenon.

Today, the inevitability of change is being noticed.

For years, the back cover of the cookbooks carried a picture of Jean, portrait-style, wearing big glasses and the suggestion of a smile. Now, more than 100 titles later, the back cover shot has begun to feature Jean Paré and friend, or friends, in which she is always pictured with at least one other person.

June 2005. "Increasingly, Mom's role is that of mentor," says Grant, sitting beside her in the company boardroom. "But she influences every action and every decision. She makes us accountable, and she always will."

Both as her son and her business partner, he sees Jean's personality, her strength of will and her unshakable faith in her family as their most valuable company asset.

"We need to figure out what you want to do next," Grant says, turning toward her, speaking son-to-mother. "We'd really like to know."

Jean looks slightly puzzled, as though the answer is so obvious that she wonders why he'd bother to ask.

Of course there's still travelling to be done, the pastry shops she still wants to visit, the one in Vienna with the high ceilings, the heavenly tortes, and the *Kaffee mit Schlag* ... Would it be Demel's? Or Sachers? Maybe both. Now that could be a fun trip ...

At almost any point, Jean can digress into topics that interest her so much these days. Places she's been, or is yet to visit, meals she remembers eating here or there, people she met ...

But her son's question is a serious one, so she gives him a thoughtful, serious answer.

"I want to stay active and involved, for as long as I can," she says firmly. "And I'm hoping we have a business here that will outlive me."

EIGHT

COFFEE AND CONVERSATIONS

Looking back isn't always easy for this family. Each of them has closed a door or two on the past, hoping never to have to re-open them. But time is a healer, and today, they're able to sit together around a table and reflect on the role their mother played in their remarkable survival as a family unit, stronger now than ever.

— Lyall Lovig —

"We're talking about a time when all the other mothers were at home. Women weren't supposed to think, but Mom thought a lot. She was in the office, balancing the books, keeping the business afloat. She was years ahead of her time."

"We're a business-oriented family. For us, doing business was fun, and for awhile, Mom and Dad were a team. All summer long, June through September, I was part of that team, working in the auction mart as a hired hand.

"In September, every Tuesday and Friday there'd be a sale, and the night before, I'd help Mom stamp burgers. She'd cut wax paper into squares, and I'd go at it — one paper, one scoop hamburger, more paper, squash the meat. Get it on the pile, make some more.

"Mom made pies. Mostly they were fresh fruit pies in season — she was running a sort of gourmet deli business through the auction mart, well ahead of her time. I'd pitch in on the pies when she needed it, but the burgers were the labour-intensive part. I must have stamped a million burgers with that wooden press."

"I remember duck-hunting season. Mom would pick me up after school and drop me off with my shotgun at Charlie Pearman's slough, six or seven miles from town. I'd sit there by myself, and maybe shoot a couple of miserable little ducks, and just at the edge of darkness, Mom would show up in her car to drive me back to town. She was totally reliable."

She was also unfailingly generous with her kids.

"She had a '62 Chevrolet Biscayne, and I had a '57 Ford Fairlane two-door hardtop, metallic blue with cruiser fender skirts. When I drove down Main Street, everybody knew I was in town. That car was *me.*

"But if I needed to go hunting, I'd borrow her car. She always said yes. Then she'd take my car downtown on some errand, and she'd get such a kick out of being seen in it, a middle-aged woman driving a car like that. Everything has always been fun with Mom."

Like his younger siblings, Lyall greatly admired his father.

"My Dad was so smart, so savvy. I used to think he had a crystal ball in his pocket, he could size up a situation fast, in a dispassionate way. They both taught me a lot about business; that it's fun, even when it doesn't succeed the way you want it to. Dad always said the only people who don't make mistakes are the ones who don't do anything, so either lead, follow or get out of the way."

But Lyall was still a kid, and for all his admiration for both parents, the bad times between them were hard on him. He often took refuge with his grandparents.

"Whenever there was a family vacation, I begged off, and got them to drop me at Grandpa Elford's farm."

As the Lovigs' family crisis deepened, Ed Elford, who had retired from the oil business to become a farmer near Ardrossan, Alberta, gradually became a father figure to all four of the Lovig kids. Clarence's drinking had left Lyall, his eldest son, with a sense of abandonment that he's never quite forgotten, and his grandfather's calm, reasonable presence was a lifeline for a confused teenage boy who wasn't quite as cool as he pretended to be.

"There was so much good before the bad. We all remember that. But what happened to my dad is something that starts slow, like a tooth decaying, and then it hurts like hell. I remember the times when we couldn't find him. That's hard on a kid. You feel all alone."

In retrospect, he sees both Clarence and Jean in a different light.

"When things started to fall apart, I got impatient with both of them. Their behaviour interfered with good business, with going and growing."

When Lyall left home to attend university in Bozeman, Montana, he liked the idea of a small college. It was also a long way from Vermilion, a small town where there were no secrets, and he may have liked that too.

Jean had mixed emotions about Lyall's decision to go so far away.

"I was happy that he wanted to get more education, but I wished he'd have stayed closer to home," she recalls. "Gail and I drove him down, but it was hard saying goodbye."

For Lyall, there was also the comforting pull of the farm, where Grandpa Elford had his cattle.

"Maybe I was a little homesick. I still get that way, even when the home (in Vermilion) isn't there anymore. There were good times there, and good memories of Dad, before the trouble."

So he came back to Canada, and moved into Grandpa Elford's four-bunk pumphouse.

"It's always been a cattle and horse thing with me. I like working with animals, and I love being outdoors."

In the summer of 1967, he bought a few cattle, and soon he had a small herd of Herefords.

"On January 1, 1968, I met this wonderful, beautiful girl in Ardrossan. Her name was Cynthia Sharhan, and I knew she was the one. She still is."

Lyall and Cynthia married, settling in the Ardrossan area. Although he always had a few cattle, Lyall also became an auctioneer, and he branched into real estate, a field that continues to fascinate him.

For a period of time, from mid-1985 until late-1993, he and Cynthia worked for Company's Coming. They were a team, he as distribution manager, she right beside him, as warehouse manager.

But Jean's eldest son has cattle in his blood, and he went back to raising red Angus, his all-time favourite beef-on-the-hoof. Although he no longer has cattle, he still loves the business.

"Those cattle were good, hard-living, honest producers. If it snows some, they don't stand at the gate bawling, they hustle for their feed. I like their independent spirit."

It's a spirit Clarence and Jean would have agreed on.

— *Brian Lovig* —

"She likely knew there was no point in trying to reason with me. It doesn't matter how much you reason with somebody who's drinking, because he won't listen, and if you get mad at him, he'll fight back. Mom already knew that. With us, she was all about caring, not criticizing."

It was probably inevitable that Brian, the second of Jean's four children, would grow up too fast.

Reflecting on his family history, he remembers the better days of Clarence Lovig.

"Dad was a traveller and an adventurer. He was stimulated by people, by business, by the deal. He liked to know what was going on over there, wherever there was. I think he was a true seeker.

"He had high expectations, and I guess he figured the drinking was a small thing and we should be big enough, we could handle it … but we're all just people, and we couldn't handle it."

As a child, Brian worshipped his dad, and hung out with him at the auction mart as much as he was allowed, spending countless hours watching Clarence work the crowds, listening to the patter, learning the ropes, mimicking the singsong routine of a good auctioneer. Clarence, always happy to provide an entertaining moment, let the boy perform.

"He wasn't babysitting," Brian says. "He'd put me up on the stage wearing a big cowboy hat, and I'd auction. It was serious business, and I felt like I was part of it."

Brian sold his first horse to rodeo promoter Harry Vold, and he has never forgotten the thrill of that initial business deal. Heady stuff for one so young, and soon he was conducting auctions. (Brian went on to become a licensed auctioneer, as did his older brother and his sister, but all the Lovig kids are experienced auctioneers.)

"Initially, the drinking didn't interfere with Dad's work, so he was usually there. He was like my best friend."

No longer just a kid pretending to be an auctioneer, Brian was now a kid selling livestock.

Small wonder that school held little charm for him, and it soon became a total drag. One day he came home and announced that he'd quit. He was fourteen.

Neither Jean nor Clarence were in favour, and both of them tried to get him to change his mind, but in reality, they no longer had any control over their second eldest son.

"I know Mom worried about it. Grandpa Elford came to see me on a couple of occasions, likely hoping to sort me out. He told me about choices. I could be an eagle, and soar. Or I could be a crow, and be nothing but a darned nuisance. It was my choice."

But at fourteen, Brian was already flying on his own wings, in his own way. He was an auctioneer, popular with the crowds, and he was working most of the time. He had his own money and a gang of like-minded pals to party with.

"I smoked, but not in front of my parents. I drank a bit because I was around a drinking crowd. But Mom always waited up for us. It kept me from drinking too much because when you're trying to sneak in at four a.m. with liquor on your breath, the last person you want to see is your mother."

When he wandered in late, Jean never lectured or threatened. She'd just be grateful he was home safe, and go quietly to bed.

At sixteen Brian had a car, and by seventeen, he had a wife and a baby.

Then something happened that made a lasting impression. His car was stolen, by some of his friends. That night, his grandfather's advice about making choices began to make sense.

"I finally realized I was making bad choices."

Gradually he managed to make better choices, and with a lot of hard work and the natural abilities he so admired in his dad, he became a successful businessman with a busy career as an auctioneer. However, along with the sociable nature and outgoing personality, Brian had acquired some of his father's other habits.

"I was never a clinical alcoholic, but I was drinking a lot, smoking heavily, gambling …

That all came to an abrupt and unexpected end the day two of his children asked him to take them to the fair.

"I was terribly hungover, but I took them anyway, and they wanted to go on one of those crazy rides. I think it's called the Tilt-A-Whirl."

He was as sick as the proverbial dog.

"That did it. At that moment, I looked at my sons and I saw very clearly that

I was doing the same thing to them that my dad had done to me. Here I was, with a beautiful wife, great kids, and I was behaving like an idiot.

"I remember realizing this: I wanted my kids to choose to be eagles, and not have me as a negative example."

That was June 21, 1978. He quit drinking; went cold turkey. He also quit smoking, quit gambling, and just for good measure, he dumped the caffeine habit — no more coffee.

Exactly one year later, on June 21, 1979, he got a phone call from Clarence, who said he had some pain in his chest, but didn't think it was serious.

The next day, he found his father lying on the bed.

He'd been dead for several hours.

— *Grant Lovig* —

"Mom is a worker bee. She spends her time doing, not directing ... Despite all the things she's done, and all the fame she's achieved, she's still Mom."

Grant is Jean's youngest son, the one who, over the years, has spent so much time with her, first as a child growing up, and then as a business partner.

"As a mother, she had rules, and limits, but she gave us a lot of freedom. How many mothers would have let their kids dig up the entire backyard and turn it into a maze of tunnels? I'm not talking about a few holes in the ground — we did some major excavating. We even had candles in jars as lights placed on the side walls for light. That's how deep it was.

"Looking back, I suppose we could have had a problem, the thing could have caved in on us, and I remember that Dad actually went out and jumped on the tunnels to be sure they were fairly safe. But Mom had a way of trusting fate, and she also credited us with a certain amount of common sense."

Grant grew up around cattle, horses, cowboys and auctioneers. During the heyday of the Vermilion Auction Mart he was too young to take an active role, and while Brian was a rodeo cowboy and Lyall was getting a start in the cattle business, Grant was still their kid brother, watching his older siblings operate in what he considered to be a much larger world.

"I remember on non-sale days, Gail and I would go to the Gainers shipping station at the auction mart and make instant coffee with plenty of Carnation evaporated milk. We'd soak sugar cubes in it, one by one, until the concoction was sweet enough to suit us. For some reason I loved doing that. It sticks in my mind."

Like his siblings, Grant remembers his mother as a busy woman who could still find time to do the things that mattered to her children.

He also gave her plenty to worry about.

Grant had a knack for getting into tight spots. There was his early encounter with a black bear during a camping trip.

"I think Mom started hitting it with her shopping bag, and Dad was swinging a pail at it, so it sauntered away."

Then there was the time he accidentally inhaled a couple of coins, getting them lodged in his windpipe. And nobody in the family will forget the time he almost drowned. He was three at the time.

"We were at Gram and Grandpa Elford's cabin at Seba Beach, about 45 minutes west of Edmonton. Mom had been checking on us, but it takes such a short time for a kid to get in trouble in water. When she found me, all she could see was a blue bathing suit bobbing in the water, bottom up, so she knew it was one of her kids. She ran through the water, trying to reach me, and she talks about reaching down and grabbing my feet, pulling me out of the water. I'd swallowed a lot of the lake, and I was lucky I didn't drown. For a year after that, I was too scared to take a bath in a regular tub, and she'd bathe me in the sink."

Grant got over his fear of water, and grew up to love water sports, including swimming, but Jean has never forgotten how close he once came to drowning.

As her children grew, Jean became adept at juggling her time to meet their individual and sometimes unusual needs.

"When I was in grade 5 at Virginia Park School in Edmonton, I volunteered her services to bake apple pies for my entire class for Valentine's Day," Grant remembers. "I had no idea how much work it would involve, I just knew they were the world's best apple pies."

Some mothers might have begged off, or made do with bakery pies, or even made tarts and called it done. But Jean wasn't like that.

"When I told her about the apple pies, she just asked how many kids there were in the class, and went out to buy apples. Then she started baking. The next afternoon, there she was at my school, with over thirty individual pies, each one with proper pastry lids."

By the time he reached high school, Grant had started moving with a faster crowd.

"There was a lot of drinking. We had big cars and we drove too fast. What are now called bush parties — we called them pasture parties — went on all summer long."

Grant had his own car, and the youngest Lovig boy soon became well acquainted with the local RCMP.

"They knew me by name," he says. "I guess Mom worried a bit, but I assured her we'd all be okay, and she believed me."

Grant remembers that his dad had a dream: to build an auction mart for each of his children to run. Although it didn't come about, Clarence did give many young auctioneers their start. Typically, they were brash, young, flashy dressers, but he had time for them, and some of them did quite well.

Would Clarence have been surprised if he could have known that Grant and Jean would eventually be in business together, a business far removed from the world of the auction ring?

Probably. There are days when even Jean seems surprised. Grant often travels with her, and he sees the Jean effect.

"We visited practically every television and radio station in Canada at one time or another. Mom is always up for an interview and keen to chat about cooking. She's especially well suited for phone-in radio programs.

"In Ottawa in the late '80s, an engineer came into the room next to the studio where I was waiting while Mom was on-air. He pointed to the phone in amazement and said, 'No one can call in or out. The phone lines are jammed with people wanting to speak with your mother!'"

"In a way, I think I'm the luckiest of Mom's kids," he muses. "She loves us all, but I'm the one who, over the years, has been able to spend so much time with her."

— *Gail Lovig* —

"My mother is unique. I've never met anyone who comes close … I came into the world with her, and I guess if I had a choice, I'd go out with her."

When she talks about her relationship with her mother, Gail's face is animated, her voice occasionally husky with emotion.

This is the woman she knows, with all her quirks and foibles.

"We all laugh because she's so incredibly punctual. She usually gets to the airport in time for the flight before her flight. She's also one of the few people I know who actually likes airline food. She loves eating on planes. She always says, 'Be sure you book a meal flight.' When the tray comes, she eats dessert first."

And then there's her fascination with ringing telephones.

"If a phone rings, she'll answer it, no matter what she's doing. The answering machine means nothing to her. At the office, if she's paged, get out of her way — she'll literally run to catch the phone, so she doesn't keep the caller waiting."

Jean has always insisted on answering all her own mail, even at times when the fan mail has been heavy, and she writes every letter by hand. She is also religious about the old-fashioned virtue of sending thank you notes. She fires off a gracious note for anything that appears in print about her, or about the company, or for any hospitality she might receive.

"Mom is frugal. She always turns off the lights when she leaves a room, and she never wastes food.

"I think it's a measure of her energy that she always wears shoes in the house. If I'm in Vermilion, sleeping upstairs, I hear her feet tapping around in the morning, and I know she's up, setting the table, getting breakfast," says Gail.

"It was always that way. She had a thing about getting up, getting dressed, getting into your day. When I was a kid, if I came to the table in my pyjamas, she'd say 'Why don't you just get dressed? It won't take a minute.'

"Mom is a born event planner. She loves every stage of party planning — the menus, the table centres, which punchbowl to use ... Hooray, another party! She loves what we call the Great Staff Gatherings. As soon as we mention any possible excuse for a gathering, whether it's a barbecue, a potluck, a dinner, anything at all, she's right in there. And there's food in every room.

"We celebrate everything. And when we come home from an event, no matter how long the day has been, or how long she's been on her feet, she'll always say, 'Anyone for a nightcap?'

"I think that celebrative side must have come from her own parents. I remember the Christmases there, with the beautifully set table, very formal, always the good china and silver, and the footed glass of tomato juice at the top right of the plate, though there was never any alcohol.

"I don't remember my grandparents being especially affectionate, certainly not with each other, and I think that was Grandma's way of showing affection — with a wonderful meal, and everybody gathered around the family table."

"One of my strongest memories? On my seventh birthday, we were living with Mom's parents, Dad had left us, and she was humiliated again. I didn't expect anything for my birthday. But she got me these wonderful Barbie dolls. I don't know how she did it. I still have them.

"The first Christmas after Dad left, Mom was really struggling to make it okay for us. I think it may have been her worst Christmas. She wrapped a lot of small things in separate packages, so it would look like more than it really was, and we'd have the excitement of opening presents.

"Brian was poking around under the tree the way kids do, checking the presents, and he saw that there was nothing for Mom, not one single gift. So he bought her a set of metal measuring spoons with a wooden holder, and on Christmas morning there they were, all wrapped up under the tree. She still has them, and she treasures them."

"I remember desperately wanting to be Red Riding Hood in the school play. I didn't get the part, so Mom made me a Red Riding Hood costume anyway, so I could wear my own cape.

"I've always loved animals, and I remember calling Mom from school one January day to come and get this tiny stray cat that was outside, freezing.

"She came, and she rescued the cat, just like I knew she would." (Today, Gail keeps the faith by rescuing cats, feeding strays at a regular time and place, rounding up as many as she can, and paying for them to be spayed or neutered.)

"I remember as a teenager, sitting up until three a.m. talking to her about God, and whether or not he was real. That's a side of her that few people ever see.

"I didn't do drugs, but I was curious, and I remember bringing hash home to show her. I think I also brought her an LSD tab for the same reason. In those days, it wasn't hard to find. Most mothers would have freaked out, but not her."

In fact, Jean's reaction to her daughter's adventurous behaviour may have been more serious than Gail remembers.

"I was worried sick when she did things like that. What if she'd been caught carrying that stuff around? She could have been charged with possession. The police might not have believed that she just wanted to take it home and show it to her mother."

Still, it didn't happen, and Gail's memory of her relationship with her mother is probably somewhat unusual for mothers and daughters, because it's entirely positive.

"Not only was she shockproof, but she trusted us," she recalls. "If I needed a ride home in the middle of the night after a party, all I had to do was call. She'd come and get me, no questions, no lectures."

"But that doesn't mean there weren't limits. She wouldn't let anybody swear in our home. That was a line I could not cross."

"I was a bad kid. Really difficult. I didn't like being a kid, and I hated school for a lot of reasons, but she taught me to believe in myself."

Jean: "She's not being fair to herself. She wasn't a bad kid at all, but she did worry me, especially when she was starting to skip school. Maybe she did hate school ... I remember that she wanted to take more subjects than she needed in one semester, so she could be finished and get out of there," says Jean, looking vaguely worried, as she often does when talking about the bad old days before her life turned around.

But then she laughs.

"For a kid who caused me so much worry, that girl turned out really well!"

Gail and Jean's close relationship hasn't changed, except that these days, instead of Jean looking after Gail, the tables have turned, at least a little.

"Mom travels a lot, but she doesn't travel alone, and whenever I can, I fly with her. That's the way I want it," she says.

"I came into the world with her, and I guess if I had a choice, I'd go out with her."

NINE

AFTER ALL

On March 1, 2005, Jean was in Palm Springs with her son Brian and his wife, Linda, when she was called to the phone.

What she heard was frightening. She felt her heart starting to race, and she swallowed hard.

"I have to go home. Right away."

Her husband, Larry Paré, the man who had been her biggest fan and travelling companion for the past thirty-six years, was gravely ill. He was taken by helicopter to a hospital in Edmonton, where he was diagnosed with an aggressive lymphoma, and quickly transferred to the Cross Cancer Clinic.

Jean flew home immediately, and disappeared inside the hospital, staying with Larry through the long days, and leaving him during the night to catch a few hours rest at her Edmonton base, a condominium she bought some years ago.

On the tenth day, Larry died.

Exhausted, Jean returned to the only solace she knew: her work and her family.

Food is one of our most basic needs, and surely one of the most pleasurable. From our first cry as we enter this world, to our last heartbeat as we leave it, and through all that comes between, food is the great sustainer of life.

Almost two centuries ago, French gastronome Jean Anthelme Brillat-Savarin insisted that we are what we eat.

If that is true, the 100-plus cookbooks that form the lifetime achievement of Jean Paré are a tangible record of Canadian history in a peculiarly tasty and user-friendly form.

This is not a new phenomenon. From the deepest well of history, the time of Confucius and Apicius, cookbooks have always told us much about ourselves. They speak about our ways of living, thinking, working, celebrating, even about our ways of worshipping.

They speak about the land we live on, and the crops we grow and harvest, each in its own season. They seek to satisfy our basic and elemental need — the need for physical nourishment — and they do it in the most comforting and sociable way.

It may be that infinite sociability that we cherish most about the work of a Jean Paré. It's part of her legacy.

Her early books celebrate the food, and food customs, of the women in her family, the mothers and grandmothers who cooked the way their mothers and grandmothers cooked.

Who among us can ever eat an old-fashioned molasses snap, or taste fresh-from-the-pot strawberry jam on a warm baking powder biscuit, without hearing the voices of those ancestral women who raised and fed the generations that came before us?

In some ways, cooking is the most transitory art, taking generations to perfect, and lasting only as long as it takes to swallow.

But it's also one of the most enduring, for the pleasure of remembered flavours and textures, and all the people, places and good times that they evoke.

This, too, is part of Jean's legacy.

It's a Tuesday in June, and the first car turns into the short lane just off Paré Drive.

Out her kitchen window, she can see across the valley where a narrow river flows, to the hills that were marked on old maps as the Hog's Back.

The women are gathering again. Jean's coffee group is a social commitment she doesn't take lightly. She never has.

These are the friends you make for a lifetime, the ones you laugh the hardest with, and the ones you hold on to when absolutely everything goes wrong.

"And when I'm not there, I know they aren't talking about me," she adds crisply.

"It's been once a week for more than three decades. An ocean of coffee! We started as three friends, and we've been as many as twelve. No rules, but we do use the good china, and we usually have two desserts."

Once, when they needed a change, they decided to go to Great Falls for coffee.

"That's in Montana. The trip took four days and three nights. And a lot of coffee."

Life hasn't been a smooth ride for Jean, though she'd tell you that the first twenty-five years and the last thirty-six have more than made up for a few bad times that came between.

There have been some truly amazing moments, at least that's how she describes them, mostly because she never expects them.

There was the night in Halifax, when she and some of her staff were in a restaurant and the waiter sailed up with a bottle of Champagne and a message from Gail: They'd just sold their one-millionth book.

"At the time, I was working on the *Desserts* book," she recalls. "I ordered every dessert on the menu!"

There have been many awards, many honours, and in 2004, when she received word that she was being made a Member of the Order of Canada, it was like icing on her cake.

"It was one of the most exciting things that's ever happened to me, professionally. There were forty-three of us taking part in the ceremony, and we had a short rehearsal — I was a little nervous — but it just rolled along."

Almost before she knew it, the moment arrived, and there she stood, with Gov. Gen. Adrienne Clarkson pinning on the rather weighty medal, with its impressive red and white ribbon.

There was a reception afterward to help them celebrate, and a banquet that night.

"Very elegant. Lovely presentation, lovely food.

"Her Honour served Canadian wine with every course. We started with seared tuna with tiny bundles of matchstick vegetables wrapped in eggplant. Then a salad, very light. Then veal tenderloin resting on the thinnest possible potato slice, with fiddleheads and white asparagus. Dessert was a delicious square with a thin chocolate curl on top, and she served Canadian ice wine with it."

Jean Paré, Member of the Order of Canada, has come a long way from the little girl pouring tea in front of her playhouse. It's been an even longer road from that desperate day when she was afraid to walk across the High Level Bridge.

She checks the coffee. It's ready, and when she opens the oven door, there's the warm, yeasty smell of fresh cinnamon buns.

Does life get any better than this moment? Probably it doesn't.

When she thinks about it, those things that matter most in life are often the simplest. Of all the good times, all the awards and the rewards, the extensive travels, even the millions of books — for her, the best time is right now, when she looks out her kitchen window and sees a familiar car rounding the drive.

The doorbell rings, and she feels that little flutter of pleasure.

It's the one she has always had, and the one she still gets, when she knows company's coming.

TEN

FROM JEAN'S KITCHEN
Favourite recipes

Abook about Jean Paré's life must include a few of the recipes that have been so much a part of her work, from the time she made her first devil's food cake through the next seven decades. These are some of her favourites.

STARTERS

"We had a coal and wood stove, and I knew if I could hold my arm in the oven for a few seconds, it was just right for a cake. If it nearly burned the fuzz off my arm, it was hot enough for a pie." (page 7)

Sour Cream Pie

"Grandma made this pie, Mom made it, I made it, and we all ground the raisins by hand using a food grinder. The first time I tasted one with whole raisins, I was surprised. I still grind them, which makes this recipe unique, but now I use a food processor. Although we made few cream pies in the early days because safe storage was a challenge, this pie is so good that there were never any leftovers to worry about."

Egg	1	1
Sour cream	1 cup	250 mL
Raisins	1 cup	250 mL
Granulated sugar	1/2 cup	125 mL
Cinnamon	1/4 tsp.	1 mL
Nutmeg	1/4 tsp.	1 mL
Allspice	1/4 tsp.	1 mL
Salt	1/8 tsp.	0.5 mL
Baking soda, just a pinch		
Unbaked 9 inch (22 cm) pie shell	1	1

Process first 9 ingredients in food processor until chunks of raisins are no longer visible.

Pour raisin mixture into pie shell. Bake on bottom rack in 350°F (175°C) oven for 35 to 40 minutes until set.

SOUR CREAM TARTS: Pour filling into unbaked tart shells until almost full. Bake on bottom rack in 400°F (205°C) oven until set. Makes 18 tarts. Especially good.

Hermits

"Everybody loves hermits. This old, old recipe got its name because the cookies taste even better if they're hidden for a day or two after baking. There was always a cookie tin full of these in our back porch, and we were allowed to eat as many as we liked — unlike iced cakes or squares, which were off limits without specific permission."

Butter or hard margarine, softened	1 cup	250 mL
Brown sugar, packed	1 1/2 cups	375 mL
Eggs	3	3
Vanilla	1 tsp.	5 mL
All-purpose flour	3 cups	750 mL
Baking powder	1 tsp.	5 mL
Baking soda	1 tsp.	5 mL
Cinnamon	1 tsp.	5 mL
Salt	1/2 tsp.	2 mL
Nutmeg	1/2 tsp.	2 mL
Allspice	1/4 tsp.	1 mL
Raisins	1 cup	250 mL
Chopped pitted dates	1 cup	250 mL
Chopped walnuts	2/3 cup	150 mL

Cream butter and brown sugar in large bowl. Beat in eggs 1 at a time. Add vanilla. Stir.

Add next 7 ingredients. Mix until no dry flour remains.

Add raisins, dates and walnuts. Mix well. Drop by heaping teaspoonfuls onto greased cookie sheets. Bake in 375°F (190°C) oven for 6 to 8 minutes until golden. Makes about 4 dozen cookies.

SALAD DAYS

Some girls might have started a hope chest, or spent hours composing lyrical prose in a five-year diary. Jean took a more practical view. She wrote her first cookbook: sat down and copied all of Ruby's best recipes into a scribbler.... "I intended to marry him," she says. "I needed my recipes."(page 19)

Simple Patty

"Mom used to fry the burgers then deglaze the pan with milk, scraping all the tasty brown bits into the gravy for flavour and colour. It's best not to use a Teflon-coated pan for this, because you won't get the delicious brown bits. This is an economical casserole, and kids love it."

Lean ground beef	2 lbs.	900 g
Dry bread crumbs	1 cup	250 mL
Water	1 cup	250 mL
Salt	2 tsp.	10 mL
Pepper	1/2 tsp.	2 mL
Dry onion flakes (optional)	2 tbsp.	30 mL
All-purpose flour	6 tbsp.	100 mL
Salt	1 tsp.	5 mL
Butter or hard margarine	4 – 6 tbsp.	60 – 100 mL
Milk	4 cups	1 L
Water	1 cup	250 mL

Combine first 6 ingredients in large bowl. Shape into 16 patties. Quickly brown both sides of patties in ungreased frying pan on medium-high. Do not cook through. Transfer browned patties to greased 3 quart (3 L) casserole.

Stir flour and salt into drippings in pan. Add 1 tbsp. (15 mL) butter at a time, stirring as it melts until flour and butter form a paste.

Slowly add milk, stirring constantly until boiling and thickened. Stir in water, scraping brown bits from bottom of pan. Pour gravy over patties in casserole. Cover. Bake in 350°F (175°C) oven for 1 hour. Serves 8.

Brown Betty

"This recipe, which is not the usual cinnamon-laced version, comes from Grandma Locke and Mom. It's so easy, and such a forgiving dish, you can give or take an apple or two. It can also be made with other seasonal fruit such as rhubarb, plums, pears or combinations of whatever fruit you have available. I like to bake it in a bigger casserole. It has a thinner base, but everybody gets some topping."

Sliced peeled cooking apple (such as McIntosh)	6 cups	1.5 L
Granulated sugar	3/4 cup	175 mL
All-purpose flour	1 1/4 cups	300 mL
Brown sugar, packed	3/4 cup	175 mL
Salt	1/2 tsp.	2 mL
Butter or hard margarine, softened	1/2 cup	125 mL

Put apple into 10 inch (25 cm) round casserole. Sprinkle granulated sugar over top.

Combine next 3 ingredients in medium bowl. Cut in butter until mixture is crumbly. Sprinkle over sugared apple. Pat down lightly. Bake, uncovered, in 375°F (190°C) oven for about 40 minutes until apple is tender. Serve with cream or ice cream. Serves 8 generously.

RHUBARB BETTY: Use sliced fresh or frozen rhubarb instead of apple, and add a touch more sugar. Better yet, add a few raisins and omit the extra sugar. Equally good.

FRESH FRUIT BETTY: Instead of apple, use sliced, peeled fresh peaches, or quartered fresh apricots.

DEEP APPLE BETTY: Sprinkle the apple with cinnamon before adding the sugar. Instead of the crumb topping, cover the apple with pie pastry. Cut slits in the pastry to allow steam to escape, and sprinkle with a bit of granulated sugar. Bake as above.

Tomato Soup Cake

"This moist, spicy cake was one of Mom's recipes, and we often used it as a sample at book fairs and trade shows. I like to make it in a big pan, which means the cake isn't as deep but you have more surface for icing."

Butter or hard margarine	1/2 cup	125 mL
Granulated sugar	1 cup	250 mL
Egg	1	1
All-purpose flour	1 1/2 cups	375 mL
Cinnamon	1/2 tsp.	2 mL
Nutmeg	1/2 tsp.	2 mL
Cloves	1/2 tsp.	2 mL
Salt	1/2 tsp.	2 mL
Raisins (optional)	1 cup	250 mL
Chopped walnuts (optional)	3/4 cup	175 mL
Hot water	2 tsp.	10 mL
Baking soda	1 tsp.	5 mL
Can of tomato soup	10 oz.	284 mL

Cream butter and sugar in large bowl. Beat in egg.

Measure next 7 ingredients into medium bowl. Mix well.

Combine hot water and baking soda in small bowl. Stir in soup. Add to butter mixture in 2 parts alternately with flour mixture in 3 parts, beginning and ending with flour mixture. Spread in greased 9 × 13 inch (22 × 33 cm) pan. Bake in 325°F (160°C) oven for 35 to 45 minutes until wooden pick inserted in centre comes out clean. Cool completely. Frost with your favourite chocolate or cream cheese icing. Cuts into 18 pieces.

IN THE SOUP

Jean is, and always has been, one hundred per cent mother, and her devotion to her children has never wavered. No matter what happened to her marriage, and no matter how wounded she felt by Clarence's behaviour, the kids came first. (page 48)

Corn Soup

"All my kids loved this soup, and still do. We like it with a good ham sandwich. Mom used a food mill to make this, and so do I, but a blender would work just as well."

Milk	3 1/2 cups	875 mL
Butter or hard margarine	1 tsp.	5 mL
Finely chopped onion (optional)	2 tbsp.	30 mL
Cans of cream-style corn (14 oz., 398 mL, each)	2	2
All-purpose flour	2 tbsp.	30 mL
Salt	1 tsp.	5 mL
Pepper	1/8 tsp.	0.5 mL
Milk	1/2 cup	125 mL

Butter, chives or parsley, for garnish

Heat first amount of milk in large heavy saucepan until hot but not boiling.

Melt butter in frying pan. Add onion. Cook until softened. Transfer to blender or food processor. Add corn. Process until smooth.

Combine next 3 ingredients in small bowl. Slowly add second amount of milk, stirring until smooth. Pour into hot milk, stirring constantly until boiling and thickened. Add corn mixture. Heat and stir until heated through.

Garnish individual servings with a dab of butter or a sprinkle of chopped chives or parsley. Makes about 7 1/2 cups (1.9 L).

Plum Pudding

"For years my mom made carrot pudding at Christmas, because it was a classic prairie recipe. She started making plum pudding because the breadcrumbs gave it a softer texture, and we all liked it better. It's an intensely aromatic pudding, and when it comes steaming out of the pot, you get a wonderful whiff of cinnamon, nutmeg and cloves. One batch of the recipe divides nicely into three 19 oz. cans for steaming. I make 15 of these smaller puddings every Christmas to give away."

Ground suet	1 cup	250 mL
Granulated sugar	1 cup	250 mL
Raisins	2 cups	500 mL
Chopped mixed glazed fruit	1 cup	250 mL
Chopped pitted dates	3/4 cup	175 mL
Diced mixed peel	1/2 cup	125 mL
All-purpose flour	1 1/4 cups	300 mL
Dry bread crumbs	1 1/4 cups	300 mL
Baking powder	2 tsp.	10 mL
Salt	1 1/4 tsp.	6 mL
Cinnamon	1 tsp.	5 mL
Nutmeg	1 tsp.	5 mL
Baking soda	1/2 tsp.	2 mL
Eggs	2	2
Milk	3/4 cup	175 mL

Combine suet and sugar in large bowl. Add next 4 ingredients. Mix well.

Add next 7 ingredients. Stir.

Beat eggs in small bowl until frothy. Stir in milk. Add to suet mixture. Stir well. Pack into greased 2 quart (2 L) pudding pan. Cover with foil and secure with butcher's string. Place on wire rack in large pot. Pour boiling water into pot until halfway up side of pudding pan. Cover and bring to a boil. Steam for 3 hours, adding more boiling water as needed. Serve with your favourite brown sugar sauce or rum sauce. Serves 12 to 15.

THE MAIN THING

One lucky day back in 1963, just when she needed it most, fate stepped in with an opportunity for Jean. It was one of those odd accidents of time and place, and although she couldn't have known it at the time, eventually that incident would redefine her life. (page 53)

Rock Cornish Hens with Wild Rice Stuffing

"Always the centre of attention on a plate, these little duffers don't hold much stuffing, so I use a teaspoon to fill them. They look especially festive if you glaze them with currant or apple jelly."

WILD RICE STUFFING

Package of long grain and wild rice mix	6 1/4 oz.	180 g
Butter or hard margarine	1/4 cup	60 mL
Chopped onion	1 cup	250 mL
Chopped celery	1/2 cup	125 mL
Finely grated carrot	1/2 cup	125 mL
Chopped fresh mushrooms	1 1/3 cups	325 mL
Poultry seasoning	1/2 tsp.	2 mL
Salt	1/2 tsp.	2 mL
Pepper	1/8 tsp.	0.5 mL
Cornish hens (about 1 lb., 454 g, each)	6	6
Paprika, sprinkle		
Melted butter, approximately	2 tbsp.	30 mL

Wild Rice Stuffing: Cook rice according to package directions.

Melt first amount of butter in frying pan. Add onion, celery and carrot. Cook until softened.

Add next 4 ingredients. Cook for another 2 minutes. Add rice. Stir.

Stuff hens. Tie with butcher's string or secure with metal skewers. Sprinkle with paprika. Put into large roasting pan. Cook, uncovered, in 400°F (205°C) oven for 30 minutes.

Brush hens with melted butter. Cook, uncovered, for another 30 to 40 minutes until fully cooked. Sprinkle with more paprika if desired. Serves 6.

Oil and Vinegar Dressing

"For my taste, commercial dressings were too oily, so I came up with this in my early catering days. Such a simple recipe, but it's also one of the most-requested. It's very economical, and a lifesaver for any large-quantity lettuce salad."

Granulated sugar	4 cups	1 L
White vinegar	3 cups	750 mL

Cooking oil, as needed

Combine sugar and vinegar in large airtight container. Stir until sugar is dissolved. It may take a few minutes. Cover and store in refrigerator. It will keep for months. Makes about 4 cups (1 L).

Drizzle a small amount of cooking oil over your salad. Toss. Use just enough cooking oil to lightly coat. Drizzle small amounts of vinegar mixture over the salad, tossing until coated and to your taste.

Homecoming Beans

"Here's a staple for picnics, reunions or any large gathering. Use plain house-brand beans, because the ingredients you're adding will smarten up the flavour of an ordinary bean. I always bake them until that brown ring appears on the edge of the pan, just above the surface."

Cans of baked beans in tomato sauce	14	14
(14 oz., 398 mL, each)		
Ketchup	4 cups	1 L
Brown sugar, packed	1 cup	250 mL
Dry onion flakes	1/2 cup	125 mL
Worcestershire sauce	2 tbsp.	30 mL

Combine all 5 ingredients in large roasting pan. Bake, uncovered, in 350°F (175°C) oven for 2 to 2 1/2 hours, stirring at halftime, until bubbling. Serves 50.

FOREIGN FLAVOURS

Once again she arrived home with numerous recipes and her own observations and notes, and proceeded to make a version of jambalaya that played well in Vermilion and wherever else her next book, *Dinners of the World*, was sold. (page 73)

Polynesian Meatballs

"When I served these at a Boxing Day open house after our first trip to Honolulu, they seemed very exotic. They're still one of my favourites for a big cocktail party, and they go fast. I like to have a sauce or two on the side."

Can of water chestnuts, drained and finely chopped	8 oz.	227 mL
Soy sauce	3 tbsp.	50 mL
Brown or granulated sugar, packed	1 tbsp.	15 mL
Garlic cloves, minced (or 1/2 tsp., 2 mL, powder)	2	2
Parsley flakes	1 tsp.	5 mL
Onion powder	1/2 tsp.	2 mL
Lean ground beef	2 lbs.	900 g
APRICOT SAUCE		
Apricot jam	1 cup	250 mL
Cider vinegar	3 tbsp.	50 mL
Paprika	1/4 tsp.	1 mL

Combine first 6 ingredients in large bowl. Add ground beef. Mix well. Shape into 1 inch (2.5 cm) balls. Place on ungreased baking sheet with sides. Bake in 375°F (190°C) oven for about 15 minutes until meatballs are fully cooked. Makes about 80 meatballs.

Apricot Sauce: Combine all 3 ingredients in small bowl. Transfer to serving bowl. Serve with meatballs for dipping. Just right!

Jambalaya

"You can't go to New Orleans without falling in love with their cooking, and jambalaya is their signature dish. This big, friendly dish soon became one of our favourites for parties. It makes a great addition to a buffet."

Cooking oil	3 tbsp.	50 mL
Chicken parts, skin removed	4 lbs.	1.8 kg
Salt, generous sprinkle		
Pepper, generous sprinkle		
Chorizo sausages or cooked ham, cut up	2 lbs.	900 g
Chopped onion	2 1/2 cups	625 mL
Chopped celery	1 cup	250 mL
Chopped green pepper	1 cup	250 mL
Garlic clove, minced (or 1/4 tsp., 1 mL, powder)	1	1
Water	4 1/3 cups	1.1 L
Chicken bouillon cubes (1/5 oz., 6 g, each)	3	3
Long grain white rice	2 1/3 cups	575 mL
Salt	1/2 tsp.	2 mL
Cayenne pepper	1/4 tsp.	1 mL

Heat cooking oil in frying pan. Add chicken. Brown on both sides. Sprinkle with salt and pepper. Transfer to plate.

Brown sausage in same pan, adding more cooking oil if needed. Transfer to another plate.

Put next 4 ingredients into pan. Cook until softened, adding more cooking oil if needed. Remove from heat.

Measure water into large pot. Add bouillon cubes. Bring to a boil, stirring until cubes are dissolved.

Add onion mixture and remaining 3 ingredients. Stir. Add chicken and sausage. Stir gently. Cover. Simmer for about 25 minutes until rice is tender and chicken is fully cooked. Add more salt, pepper and cayenne pepper to taste. Serves 8.

Neufchâtel Cheese Fondue

"When Amanda was living in Switzerland, her host mother, Monique, invited us for a meal. We had sampled a cheese fondue in a restaurant in Geneva, but Monique's was better. She always recommended a glass of carbonated water, at room temperature, to help digest the cheese."

Dry (or alcohol-free) white wine	1/2 cup	125 mL
Garlic clove, minced (or 1/4 tsp., 1 mL, powder)	1	1
Grated Gruyère cheese	2 cups	500 mL
Grated Neufchâtel cheese	2 cups	500 mL
Cornstarch	4 tsp.	20 mL
Kirsch liqueur (optional)	1 tbsp.	15 mL
Nutmeg, sprinkle		
Pepper, sprinkle		

Combine wine and garlic in large saucepan. Heat on medium until boiling.

Put both cheeses into medium bowl. Sprinkle with cornstarch. Toss until coated. Add to wine mixture in 3 or 4 additions, stirring after each addition until cheese is melted.

Stir in kirsch, nutmeg and pepper. Carefully pour into fondue pot. Place over low heat. Makes about 2 cups (500 mL).

Note: If you can't find Neufchâtel cheese in your grocery store, Vacherin Fribourgeois or Appenzeller cheeses are equally good options.

Suggested Dippers: An assortment of bread cubes or cooked vegetables such as broccoli, cauliflower or carrots.

JUST DESSERT

As it is with many cookbooks that are essentially collections of favourite dishes, Jean's first book would be a slice of personal history, inspired by remembered flavours and aromas forever tied to time and place. (page 76)

Neapolitan Squares

"These were a great favourite with my husband Larry Paré. They keep well, and look good on a plate with other squares. They cut best on the second or third day."

BOTTOM LAYER		
Butter or hard margarine	1/2 cup	125 mL
Graham cracker crumbs	1 1/4 cups	300 mL
Brown sugar, packed	1/2 cup	125 mL
All-purpose flour	1/3 cup	75 mL
SECOND LAYER		
Medium unsweetened coconut	2 cups	500 mL
Can of sweetened condensed milk	11 oz.	300 mL
ICING		
Icing (confectioner's) sugar	2 cups	500 mL
Butter or hard margarine, softened	1/4 cup	60 mL
Maraschino cherry juice	3 tbsp.	50 mL

Bottom Layer: Melt butter in medium saucepan. Stir in graham crumbs, brown sugar and flour. Press into ungreased 9 × 9 inch (22 × 22 cm) pan. Bake in 350°F (175°C) oven for 10 minutes.

Second Layer: Combine coconut and condensed milk in medium bowl. Do this just before spreading so the coconut doesn't have time to soak up the milk. It will spread more easily. Spread on bottom layer. Bake for about 20 minutes until just starting to brown at edges of pan. Cool completely.

Icing: Beat all 3 ingredients in small bowl until smooth and light, adding more juice or icing sugar if needed until spreading consistency. Spread on cooled bars. For easier cutting, cover tightly and store for at least a day to soften. Cuts into 36 squares.

Note: If you don't have cherry juice on hand, use same amount of water plus a bit of red food colouring and 1/4 tsp. (1 mL) cherry or almond extract.

Frieda's Number 89

"The day we photographed all the squares for the first cookbook, each one had a number, so the photographer wouldn't get them mixed up. This cranberry spice bar was number 89, and when we called the neighbours in to share the squares, Frieda refused to let this one go. The recipe has borne her name ever since."

Butter or hard margarine, softened	1/4 cup	60 mL
Granulated sugar	1/2 cup	125 mL
Brown sugar, packed	1/2 cup	125 mL
Egg	1	1
Sour cream	1/4 cup	60 mL
Vanilla	1 tsp.	5 mL
All-purpose flour	1 cup	250 mL
Baking powder	1 tsp.	5 mL
Salt	1/4 tsp.	1 mL
Cinnamon	1/4 tsp.	1 mL
Coarsely chopped fresh or frozen cranberries	1/2 cup	125 mL
Chopped walnuts	1/2 cup	125 mL
Coarsely chopped peeled cooking apple (such as McIntosh)	1/2 cup	125 mL
TOPPING		
Granulated sugar	1 tbsp.	15 mL
Cinnamon	1/2 tsp.	2 mL

Cream butter and both sugars in medium bowl. Beat in egg. Add sour cream and vanilla. Stir.

Add next 4 ingredients. Stir.

Add cranberries, walnuts and apple. Mix well. Spread in greased 9 x 9 inch (22 x 22 cm) pan.

Topping: Combine sugar and cinnamon in small bowl. Sprinkle over batter in pan. Bake in 350°F (175°C) oven for about 30 minutes until wooden pick inserted in centre comes out clean. Cuts into 36 squares.

Grant's Special

"When Grant came home raving about Brent's mom's terrific squares, I told him to get the recipe, and he did. It's also called 'Seafoam Chews,' but in our family it's always been known as Grant's Special."

BOTTOM LAYER

All-purpose flour	2 cups	500 mL
Granulated sugar	1/2 cup	125 mL
Brown sugar, packed	1/2 cup	125 mL
Butter or hard margarine, softened	1/2 cup	125 mL
Milk	3 tbsp.	50 mL
Egg yolks	2	2
Baking powder	2 tsp.	10 mL
Baking soda	1 tsp.	5 mL
Salt	1/2 tsp.	2 mL
Vanilla	1 tsp.	5 mL

SECOND LAYER

Semi-sweet chocolate chips	1 cup	250 mL

THIRD LAYER

Egg whites, room temperature	2	2
Brown sugar, packed	1 cup	250 mL

TOP LAYER

Chopped salted peanuts	3/4 cup	175 mL

Bottom Layer: Mix all 10 ingredients in large bowl until crumbly. Press into ungreased 9 x 9 inch (22 x 22 cm) pan. This layer will be quite high.

Second Layer: Sprinkle chocolate chips over bottom layer.

Third Layer: Beat egg whites in small bowl until frothy. Add brown sugar in 3 additions, beating after each addition until combined. Beat until stiff. Carefully spread on chocolate chips.

Top Layer: Scatter peanuts over egg white. Press lightly so they will stick, otherwise they tend to fall off when baked. Bake in 350°F (175°C) oven for 35 minutes. Cool. For easier cutting, cover the pan to soften the meringue. Cuts into 36 squares.

ICING ON THE CAKE

Of course there's still travelling to be done, the pastry shops she still wants to visit, the one in Vienna with the high ceilings, the heavenly tortes, and the *Kaffee mit Schlag* ... (page 103)

Chiffon Cake

"This was a very new kind of cake when I began making it. Although it resembled an angel food cake in appearance, it had more substance and could be cut into many more wedges. Pink icing with pink animal holders for coloured candles topped it off. No birthday was complete without one."

Sifted cake flour	2 cups	500 mL
Granulated sugar	1 1/2 cups	375 mL
Baking powder	1 tbsp.	15 mL
Salt	1 tsp.	5 mL
Egg yolks, room temperature	7	7
Cold water	3/4 cup	175 mL
Cooking oil	1/2 cup	125 mL
Vanilla	2 tsp.	10 mL
Lemon extract	1 tsp.	5 mL
Egg whites, room temperature	7	7
Cream of tartar	1/2 tsp.	2 mL

Wash 10 inch (25 cm) angel food tube pan in hot soapy water to ensure it is completely grease-free. Measure sifted flour into large bowl. Sift again with sugar, baking powder and salt. Make a well in centre.

Add next 5 ingredients to well. Don't beat yet. Set aside.

Beat egg whites and cream of tartar in another large bowl until stiff peaks form. Set aside. Using same beaters, beat flour mixture until smooth. Slowly add to egg white, folding in mixture with a rubber spatula. Do not stir. Pour into angel food tube pan. Bake in 325°F (160°C) oven for 55 minutes. Increase heat to 350°F (175°C). Bake for another 10 to 15 minutes until wooden pick inserted in centre of cake comes out clean. Invert pan. Let stand until cake is cooled completely. Remove from pan and frost with your favourite butter icing. Cuts into 16 wedges.

Devil's Food Cake

"This cake was a favourite of my dad's. He would ask me to make it, complete with a date filling, for every meeting he had. He praised it every time, so it then became a real pleasure to make it for him. He also liked a jam filling now and then."

Sifted cake flour	2 cups	500 mL
Baking soda	1 tsp.	5 mL
Salt	1/4 tsp.	1 mL
Butter or hard margarine, softened	1/2 cup	125 mL
Brown sugar, packed	1 1/4 cups	300 mL
Eggs	2	2
Unsweetened chocolate baking squares	3	3
(1 oz., 28 g, each), melted		
Vanilla	1 tsp.	5 mL
Milk	1 cup	250 mL
CHOCOLATE ICING		
Icing (confectioner's) sugar	2 1/2 cups	625 mL
Cocoa, sifted if lumpy	1/2 cup	125 mL
Butter or hard margarine, softened	6 tbsp.	100 mL
Milk or water	1/4 cup	60 mL
Vanilla	1 tsp.	5 mL
DATE FILLING		
Chopped pitted dates	1 cup	250 mL
Water	1/2 cup	125 mL
Granulated sugar	1/4 cup	60 mL
Lemon juice	1 tsp.	5 mL
Vanilla	1/2 tsp.	2 mL

(continued on next page)

Measure sifted flour into small bowl. Sift again 3 times with baking soda and salt. Set aside.

Cream butter and brown sugar in large bowl. Beat in eggs 1 at a time. Add chocolate and vanilla. Beat well.

Add milk to butter mixture in 2 parts alternately with flour mixture in 3 parts, beginning and ending with flour mixture. Pour into 2 greased 8 inch (20 cm) round pans. Bake in 350°F (175°C) oven for 25 to 30 minutes until wooden pick inserted in centre of cake comes out clean. Cool completely.

Chocolate Icing: Beat all 5 ingredients in medium bowl until smooth and light, adding more milk or icing sugar if needed until spreading consistency. Makes about 2 cups (500 mL). Set aside.

Date Filling: Put first 4 ingredients into small saucepan. Simmer, stirring often, until mushy, adding a bit more water if needed to soften the dates. Mixture should be thick and spreadable like jam. Remove from heat.

Add vanilla. Stir well. Makes about 3/4 cup (175 mL). Fill cake and frost with chocolate icing. Cuts into 16 wedges.

COFFEE AND CONVERSATIONS

Like his siblings, Grant remembers his mother as a busy woman who could still find time to do the things that mattered to her children. (page 111)

Brownies

"This was one of Mom's favourites, and it remains one of mine, even though she made hers with melted chocolate and I use cocoa instead. This is our standard gift for media appearances, because it travels so well and we can cut it in the hotel room. Besides, what could be better than something chocolate?"

Butter or hard margarine	1/2 cup	125 mL
Cocoa, sifted if lumpy	1/4 cup	60 mL
Eggs	2	2
Granulated sugar	1 cup	250 mL
All-purpose flour	3/4 cup	175 mL
Chopped walnuts	1/2 cup	125 mL
Salt	1/8 tsp.	0.5 mL
ICING		
Icing (confectioner's) sugar	1 1/3 cups	325 mL
Cocoa, sifted if lumpy	1/3 cup	75 mL
Butter or hard margarine, softened	3 tbsp.	50 mL
Prepared strong coffee or water	1 1/2 tbsp.	25 mL

Heat butter and cocoa in small saucepan, stirring occasionally, until butter is melted. Remove from heat.

Beat eggs in medium bowl until frothy. Add next 4 ingredients. Don't stir yet. Pour cocoa mixture over top. Stir well. Spread in greased 8 x 8 inch (20 x 20 cm) pan. Bake in 350°F (175°C) oven for 25 to 30 minutes until edges start to pull away from sides of pan and wooden pick inserted in centre comes out moist but not wet with batter.

Icing: Beat all 4 ingredients in medium bowl until smooth and light, adding more coffee or icing sugar if needed until spreading consistency. Spread on warm brownies. Let stand until icing is set before cutting. Cuts into 25 squares.

Jiffy Cinnamon Rolls

"I often say, something this good shouldn't be so easy. They smell wonderful coming out of the oven, and they're so fast. Serve them warm, with coffee."

All-purpose flour	2 cups	500 mL
Granulated sugar	2 tbsp.	30 mL
Baking powder	4 tsp.	20 mL
Salt	1 tsp.	5 mL
Cold butter or hard margarine	1/4 cup	60 mL
Cold milk	1 cup	250 mL
FILLING		
Butter or hard margarine, softened	1/3 cup	75 mL
Brown sugar, packed	1 cup	250 mL
Cinnamon	1 tbsp.	15 mL
Currants or chopped raisins	1/3 cup	75 mL
GLAZE		
Icing (confectioner's) sugar	1/2 cup	125 mL
Milk or water		

Grease 12 muffin cups. Set aside. Combine first 4 ingredients in large bowl. Cut in butter until mixture is crumbly. Make a well in centre.

Add milk to well. Stir until soft dough forms, adding a bit more milk if needed. Turn out onto lightly floured surface. Knead 8 to 10 times. Roll out into 1/3 inch (1 cm) thick rectangle, 12 inches (30 cm) long.

Filling: Cream butter and brown sugar in small bowl. Add cinnamon. Stir. Spoon 1 tsp. (5 mL) into each muffin cup. Spread remaining cinnamon mixture on dough. Sprinkle currants over top. Roll up from 1 long side, jelly roll-style. Press seam against roll to seal. Cut into 12 slices. Place, cut-side down, in prepared muffin cups. Bake in 400°F (205°C) oven for 20 to 25 minutes until golden. Immediately invert onto large platter or tray. Cool completely.

Glaze: Measure icing sugar into small bowl. Stir in enough milk to make a thin glaze. Drizzle over rolls. Makes 12 cinnamon rolls.

AFTER ALL

There have been some truly amazing moments, at least that's how she describes them, mostly because she never expects them. (page 119)

Shrimp Cocktail

"In our family, this is a tradition, served at every holiday meal from Thanksgiving through Easter as well as on other special occasions. It's a little different, because my sauce has apples in it. I like to add a couple of Ritz crackers on the side."

Shredded iceberg lettuce	1 1/2 cups	375 mL
Can of medium shrimp, rinsed and drained, a few reserved for garnish	4 oz.	113 g
Chili sauce	3/4 cup	175 mL
Diced peeled cooking apple (such as McIntosh)	1/2 cup	125 mL
Finely chopped celery	1/4 cup	60 mL
Lemon juice	2 tsp.	10 mL
Onion powder	1/2 tsp.	2 mL
Salt	1/4 tsp.	1 mL
Worcestershire sauce	1/4 – 1 tsp.	1 – 5 mL

Put lettuce into 4 to 6 sherbet glasses. Place shrimp on top.

Combine next 6 ingredients in small bowl. Add 1/4 tsp. (1 mL) Worcestershire sauce. Stir. Add more to taste. Spoon over shrimp in glasses. Garnish with reserved shrimp. Serves 4 to 6.

Note: You may wish to use a shrimp ring instead of canned shrimp for a convenient, economical alternative.

Rich Tea Biscuits

"These are so easy, and so handy. I use them with stew, or as a base for strawberry shortcake. If you need just one more item to complete a meal, these are fast, and nobody can resist a hot biscuit. The fat content may be cut in half if desired for any of the following. Be sure to try them all."

All-purpose flour	2 cups	500 mL
Granulated sugar	2 tbsp.	30 mL
Baking powder	4 tsp.	20 mL
Salt	1 tsp.	5 mL
Cream of tartar	1/2 tsp.	2 mL
Cold butter or hard margarine	1/2 cup	125 mL
Cold milk	3/4 cup	175 mL

Combine first 5 ingredients in medium bowl. Cut in butter until mixture is crumbly.

Slowly add milk, stirring constantly until soft dough forms. Turn out onto lightly floured surface. Knead 8 to 10 times. Roll or pat into 1/2 to 3/4 inch (1.2 to 2 cm) thickness. The dough should be about half as thick as you want the baked product to be. Cut out circles with 3 inch (7.5 cm) biscuit cutter. Place on greased baking sheet. For soft sides, arrange just touching. For crisp sides, arrange about 1 inch (2.5 cm) apart. Bake in 450°F (230°C) oven for 12 to 15 minutes until golden. Makes about 10 biscuits.

Note: Brushing the biscuits with milk before baking will produce pretty brown tops.

BISCUIT TOPPING: Place biscuits, just touching, on hot casserole. Bake in 425°F (220°C) oven for 20 to 25 minutes.

GRAHAM BISCUITS: Reduce flour to 1 1/2 cups (375 mL) and add 1 cup (250 mL) graham cracker crumbs. A distinctive flavour.

PIZZA CRUST: Make dough as directed. Press into greased 12 inch (30 cm) pizza pan.

BUTTERMILK BISCUITS: Reduce baking powder to 2 tsp. (10 mL) and add 1/2 tsp. (2 mL) baking soda. Use buttermilk instead of milk.

TOMATO BISCUITS: Use tomato juice instead of milk. Add 1/2 cup (125 mL) grated sharp Cheddar cheese for extra flavour.

ORANGE BISCUITS: Add 1 tbsp. (15 mL) grated orange peel, and replace half of the milk with orange juice. Dip sugar cubes into more orange juice and press on top of the biscuits before baking.

Chow Chow

"Grandma Locke and my mother both made this, so I suspect it originated in the Maritimes. It's an old, old recipe — Grandma's called for a peck of tomatoes. I make about 24 jars every year and use them as gifts. Grant always says, 'When in doubt, add Chow Chow.'"

Onions	5 lbs.	2.3 kg
Very firm green tomatoes	16 lbs.	7.2 kg
Salt	1 cup	250 mL
Granulated sugar	5 lbs.	2.3 kg
Turmeric	1 1/2 – 2 tbsp.	25 – 30 mL
Pickling spice (tied in cheesecloth)	3/4 cup	175 mL
White vinegar	6 – 8 cups	1.5 – 2 L

Cut onions into quarters, then into 1/4 inch (6 mm) slices. Remove stem end from tomatoes. Cut tomatoes into quarters, then into 1/4 inch (6 mm) slices. Slicing the tomatoes after the onions will remove the onion's odour from your hands. Layer tomato and onion in large heavy preserving kettle, sprinkling each layer with salt. Cover. Let stand overnight.

Drain vegetables well. Add sugar and turmeric. Stir. Push spice bag down into vegetable mixture. Add enough vinegar until it is barely visible around edge of kettle. Too much vinegar will make too much juice. Bring to a boil, stirring often. Simmer, uncovered, for 2 hours, stirring occasionally. Discard spice bag. Adjust sugar to taste, and add more turmeric if needed to make a pleasing colour. Pour into clean sterilized jars. Seal. For added assurance against spoilage, you may choose to process in a boiling water bath. Makes about 10 quarts (10 L), or the equivalent in small jars.

Note: Do not use an enamel container. Chow Chow will scorch the bottom.

COMPLIMENTS TO A COOK

Jean Paré is of a generation that lives by what some might consider to be old-fashioned virtues. One is modesty. Another is humility. You will never hear her talk about her own accomplishments. It isn't in her nature to do so. Yet here they are, in concise lists. Her biography could not be complete without them.

Company's Coming cookbooks by Jean Paré – the first 25 years

1981	150 Delicious Squares	**1996**	Fish & Seafood
1982	Casseroles		Breads
1983	Muffins & More		Company's Coming
1984	Salads		for Christmas
1985	Appetizers	**1997**	Beef Today!
1986	Desserts		Meatless Cooking
1987	Soups & Sandwiches		Beans & Rice
	Holiday Entertaining		Ground Beef
1988	Cookies		Sauces & Marinades
	Jean Paré's Favourites		Kids Only — Snacks
1989	Vegetables		Cooking for Two
	Main Courses		The Family Table
1990	Pasta		Pint Size Beverages
	Cakes	**1998**	30-Minute Meals
1991	Barbecues		Make-Ahead Salads
	Dinners of the World		No-Bake Desserts
1992	Lunches		Breakfasts & Brunches
	Pies		Low-Fat Cooking
1993	Light Recipes		Company's Coming for
	Pint Size Buffets		Kids — Lunches
	Pint Size Finger Food		Slow Cooker Recipes
	Pint Size Party Planning		Easy Entertaining
	Microwave Cooking	**1999**	Low-Fat Pasta
1994	Preserves		Pizza!
	Light Casseroles		Biscuits, Muffins & Loaves
	Pint Size Baking Delights		Dips, Spreads & Dressings
1995	Chicken, Etc.		One-Dish Meals
	Kids Cooking		Millennium Edition
	Pint Size Chocolate		Starters

146

2000	Grilling
	Stir-Fry
	Sandwiches & Wraps
	Soups & Salads
	Kids Cook! After-School Snacks
	Kids Cook! Bag Lunches
	Kids Cook! Weekend Treats
	Make-Ahead Meals
	Chocolate Everything
	The Potato Book
2001	Diabetic Cooking
	Appliance Cooking
	Greatest Hits Italian
	Greatest Hits Mexican
	Cook for Kids
	Gifts from the Kitchen
	Stews, Chilies & Chowders
	Fondues
2002	The Beef Book
	Asian Cooking
	Cooking for the Seasons
	The Cheese Book
	The Rookie Cook
	Rush-Hour Recipes
	Home for the Holidays
	Sweet Cravings
2003	Heart-Friendly Cooking
	Year-Round Grilling
	Weekend Cooking

	Garden Greens
	Chinese Cooking
	The Pork Book
	Decadent Desserts
	Most Loved Appetizers
2004	Recipes for Leftovers
	Diabetic Dinners
	Most Loved Main Courses
	The Egg Book
	School Days Parties
	Herbs & Spices
	Baking — Simple to Sensational
	The Beverage Book
	Most Loved Treats
2005	Slow Cooker Dinners
	Low-Carb Recipes
	Most Loved Barbecuing
	30-Minute Weekday Meals
	School Days Lunches
	Easy Healthy Recipes
	Potluck Dishes
	Christmas Gifts from the Kitchen
	Most Loved Cookies
2006	*(January to April)*
	Ground Beef Recipes
	Most Loved Salads & Dressings
	Timeless Recipes for All Occasions

Honours and awards presented to Jean over the years

1990–91	Ernst & Young Entrepreneur of the Year Award
1992	Fraser Milner Casgrain LLP Pinnacle Award
1996	Global's Woman of Vision Award
1997	YWCA Women of Distinction Award
2003	Queen Elizabeth Golden Jubilee Medal
2004	Junior Achievement Alberta Business Hall of Fame
2004	Member of the Order of Canada
2004	Cuisine Canada certificate for special achievement in Canadian Culinary Publishing
2004	Pharmasave's Remarkable Woman Award
2004	Growing Alberta Distinguished Service Award
2005	Rotary Integrity Award
2005	Canadian Sales Hall of Fame